W9-BLF-693

How to
Drug-Proof
Kids

A PARENTS' GUIDE TO
EARLY PREVENTION

Text by Jodi Freeman   Illustrations by Terry Flanagan
The Think Shop, Inc.
P.O.Box 3754; Albuquerque, NM 87190-3754;
(505) 298-9168

How to Drug-Proof Kids:
A Parents' Guide to Early Prevention, First Edition.
Text by Jodi Freeman. Illustrations by Terry Flanagan.

Published by: The Think Shop, Inc.
                P.O.Box 3754
                Albuquerque, NM 87190-3754
                (505) 298-9168

Library of Congress Cataloging in Publication Data:
Freeman, Jodi
     How to Drug-Proof Kids: A Parents' Guide to Early
     Prevention
1. non-fiction
2. substance abuse prevention
3. mental health
LC 87-051410

ISBN 0-937871-32-X softcover

DEDICATION

This book is dedicated to all my great teachers of life: Lew Johnson, Bill Walseth, Ardis Collins, Carol Homer, Bob Fetsch, Scott Morton, Dale Frank, Vonda Long, and Brian Freeman. Without these people, I would not know all the important things I have learned — and this book would not have been possible.

And this book is dedicated to you. It is not chance that you are reading this book. You have it because you care a great deal about kids. You want them to learn to be all that they can be. The skills in this book are some of the most relevant to a happy successful life.

— Jodi Freeman

TABLE OF CONTENTS

LIFE SKILLS FOR DRUG PREVENTION

QUOTATIONS FROM DRUG USERS AND COUNSELORS
(With more activities for children)

THE GOAL

DRUG INFORMATION

RESOURCES FOR FURTHER INFORMATION . . .

WARNING – DISCLAIMER

This book offers no guarantees, either expressed or implied, that your children will never touch tobacco, alcohol, or drugs. The only purpose is to offer guidelines as to what works best in substance abuse prevention. You can not control the choices children make, and neither can the authors or the publisher. Since only the children control their own choices, the best you can do is to provide them with opportunities to develop life skills that will make the need for drugs obsolete.

This book will not prevent your kids from experimenting with drugs. The *only* thing that can do that is your *direct* participation in their lives. This book is designed to help you do that in the most effective ways possible.

Should you have even the slightest suspicion that your child might already be experimenting with tobacco, alcohol, or drugs, the most important thing you can do is get outside professional help. Remember, it's hard to see the picture when you're in the frame.

The fastest road to improvement is with the assistance of a professional trained in dealing with substance abuse. You wouldn't rely on yourself and your friends to remove your child's tonsils, and this is much more serious. Time is critical. Every day you delay getting help, the chances of full recovery decrease. (Even if you are a drug abuse therapist, outside help is essential!) Talk to your school counselor (free), local mental health center (which may have a sliding scale for fees), or look in the Yellow Pages under *drug abuse treatment*. Do it now.

Every effort has been made to make this book as complete and as accurate as possible. However, there may be mistakes, both typographical and in content. Therefore, this text should be used only as a general guide and not as an ultimate source of substance abuse prevention information. Furthermore, this book contains information on substance abuse prevention only up to the printing date.

The purpose of this book is to educate and entertain. The author and The Think Shop, Incorporated shall have neither liability nor responsibility to any person or entity with respect to any loss or damage caused or alleged to be caused directly or indirectly by the information contained in this book.

WARNING – DISCLAIMER

FOREWORD

Most everyone today agrees that drugs are a major problem in the United States, threatening our kids and our future. Drug abuse has become a significant issue in presidential politics. Congress has made repeated attempts to turn the tide of drug abuse in this country through directed funding of countermeasures. Yet we seem to be losing the battle as the 1980's draw to a close. Politicians and a cover story of Time magazine seriously discuss whether the major drugs of abuse should be legalized — a kind of unconditional surrender in the war on drugs.

No major public health problem or disease has ever been conquered by treatment alone. Though the need for ministering to victims is painfully clear and important, our treatment and even law enforcement efforts are rather like fishing drowning people out of a fast-flowing river. Some we can save. Some are nearly dead by the time we catch them. Many will wash by us as we watch helplessly. To our amazement and frustration, some who are pulled ashore turn and plunge back into the current — perhaps to be saved further downstream before the waterfall, perhaps not.

It is increasingly clear that in order to stop this suffering and wasting of lives, some of us will have to head upstream and find out why and how our children are getting into the river in the first place. It is likely to be a long journey, but we seem to have no other choice. Further upstream, where the river is narrower and the current not so swift, we have a better chance of pulling people out before they are swept up in the dizzying rush of the rapids. Still further upstream, perhaps we will find the places where they are falling, jumping, or being pushed into the water.

That is our task for the future: prevention. Though many offer to sell us maps of the terrain and solutions to the problem, the fact remains that at this point we simply aren't sure how to prevent drug abuse effectively. Yet we want to do something. The advice to "Just say no!" sounds good, but somehow we suspect that it is far too simplistic, and perhaps most unrealistic for those kids who are at the highest risk of drug abuse. "Just say no!" is not a method, but a goal—our destination upstream. How do we get there?

It is at this point that the value of a contribution like Jodi Freeman's *How to Drug-Proof Kids* becomes apparent. In the field of drug abuse prevention we are, at present, greatly in need of alternatives and possibilities. This well-written book is filled with them— hundreds of ideas, tips, activities, and options. It is a creative menu from which schools, programs, and families may choose the items that seem most appropriate for their own situations. Ultimately, of course, we will need to test ideas such as these scientifically, to make sure that they do prevent problems. As Freeman rightly points out, some of our past efforts to prevent have even backfired, increasing use and abuse. For now, we need new ideas to test.

There are several aspects of this book which I particularly like. First, though the topic is a deadly serious one, many of the items on the menu are fun activities to be shared by children and the adults who care about them. Somehow we need to get beyond the terrible facts and the dread we feel if we are to speak in the language of children.

Yet there is no attempt to disguise the seriousness of the problem, and a second admirable quality of Freeman's work is her consistent admonition to tell the truth to children. They are daily bathed in lies (or at least partial truths—a more dangerous kind of lie) about drugs. Peers and media programming give the message that using drugs (including tobacco and alcohol) is fun. That is true in part, but it is not the whole truth. Missing is the rest of the story—that there are much safer ways to have fun than swimming just upstream from the rapids. Daily our children are told through advertisements that cigarettes, chewing tobacco, and alcohol are symbols of adulthood, the marks of sophistication, wealth, sexuality, popularity, health (!), strength, liberation, and success. Those downstream know the truth, but often too late. Even the endless commercial for over-the-counter medications give us the message: Don't endure discomfort even for a moment — take something and feel better. Whatever else we do in our prevention programming, it is essential that we tell our children (and ourselves) the truth.

A third valuable aspect of this book is the range of practical options it provides. Telling children "Just say no," is a bit like telling overweight people, "Just lose weight." The question is how. The approaches described here focus on multiple targets: self-esteem, skills for communication and resistance, family ties, and analyzing persuasion strategies used to influence us. No one of these is the answer. Effective prevention efforts will likely combine a variety of strategies, and Freeman offers a broad menu of options.

Finally, Freeman's perspective is a refreshing and truthful recognition that "drugs" include, in a very central way, tobacco and alcohol. It has long been recognized that these popular and legal drugs represent a gateway to the illicit drugs. Virtually no one abuses marijuana, cocaine, hallucinogens, or narcotics without having first — often at a young age — become acquainted with alcohol and/or tobacco. These widely-advertised and promoted substances are our gateway drugs, and they deserve center stage in any program that intends to stem the tide of drug abuse.

Until we confront the fact that we are a drug-oriented society, prone to escape discomfort by chemical means — until we address our widespread acceptance and active promotion of the legal drugs, we are unlikely to make much headway in combating drug abuse as a whole. The immensely profitable nature of drug dealing makes it almost impossible to cut off supply, though we should not stop trying. Our alternative is to head upstream, and do all that we can to reserve the demand for drugs, both legal and illicit. In the process we may have to face some unpleasant realities about our society and ourselves.

I could go on. There is much to say about how important it is to prevent drug abuse and how that might be accomplished. But this book is already brimming with ideas. I'll just stop here, so you and I can both get ideas about the important business of trying out some of these ideas with our children.

William R. Miller, Ph.D.
Professor of Psychology and Psychiatry
Director of Clinical Training
The University of New Mexico

ABOUT THIS BOOK

This book has activities and discussion topics that are appropriate for all ages of children. These materials are not assigned age or grade levels, as only you know what is most appropriate for your children. There are twelve year olds who still love children's books and cutesy cartoons, and others who are much too busy with sex and drugs to be interested in such juvenile things. Many of the activities and topics for discussion are appropriate with any age child who is old enough to talk. Modifications can be made to fit your children's interest.

There is no script for you to use. One of the most important skills to be practiced is communication—listening and responding appropriately to what you hear. There is no script that can predict what your children will say or feel. Everyone will benefit most from a free exchange of thoughts and feelings.

This material will get you started in the right direction to drug-proof kids. References are given to other books if you want to teach kids more about a specific skill.

The author currently works in the public schools and would very much like to see any of the children's work or comments about these lessons. This will help improve the next edition of the book, and who knows? Your children's work might be included (with parental permission only). Feel free to write, in care of the publisher. All responses will be answered (unless we're totally overwhelmed.)

This book uses the generic pronouns he, him, and his to also include the female gender. The only purpose is to make the reading easier. "Ask him if he wants his paper" is much easier to read than "Ask him or her if he or she wants his or her paper"!

This is not a macho attitude, as the author is a quite liberated woman who believes a real woman can use any pronouns she wants!

AN UNPOPULAR PHILOSOPHY

How to Drug-Proof Kids teaches children they don't need drugs, not even tobacco and alcohol. If children don't use these "gateway drugs", it is extremely unlikely they will touch illegal drugs. Almost every drug user started with tobacco and alcohol.

This is drug prevention, not drug education. It is not intended to teach children about the horrors of drugs (which historically has increased drug usage). The purpose is to give kids the life skills to be able to say no to the "gateway drugs" (tobacco and alcohol) as well as illegal drugs and other forms of substance abuse.

Saying "no" isn't always easy. When was the last time you were talked into something you really didn't want? Last month? Last week? This morning? We are surrounded by influences and demands that we didn't request...the person selling you aluminum siding, the ads that get you to buy "just one more thing" on your overloaded credit card, subscribing to a magazine you won't read, surprising your own kid with that special "whatever" that he had his heart set on...the list goes on. We all have our weak areas where saying "no" is difficult, even though we know we should.

But the things most of us give in to are merely annoying. They do not risk ruining or endangering our lives.

If we want to save kids who are at risk for using drugs, we must meet the needs that cause the risk. We must help children develop positive self-concepts, assertiveness, critical thinking skills, develop positive self-concepts, assertiveness, critical thinking skills, decision-making skills, coping skills, plus give them the facts about the dangers of substance abuse.

Children must learn that they have options. What is offered to them is not their only choice. With good critical thinking and decision-making skills, children can evaluate and decide what is in their best interest. With assertiveness and a healthy self-concept, children will say no to the resulting peer pressure and successfully deal with the temporary left-out feelings that may follow.

The rationale for this approach is obvious if one just looks at the continued use of tobacco and the drinking-and-driving problem. Everyone knows the facts, but did everyone suddenly decide to stop poisoning their lungs and/or endangering the lives of themselves and others? Scare tactics just don't work, even when they're undeniably true!

Many people think if we could just stop drug traffic, it would solve all our drug problems. It's not that simple.

WARNING!

THE INFORMATION IN THE NEXT PARAGRAPH IS NOT TO BE GIVEN TO CHILDREN! THEY HAVE ENOUGH IDEAS ALREADY, AND IF YOU ARE A TEACHER, YOU COULD BE SUED!

Before kids have access to drugs, they start sniffing glue, correction fluid, paint, or gasoline. They drink cough medicine for its alcohol. They take prescription and/or over-the-counter medications. They get cigarettes and "chew." They sniff the gas in empty spray cans of whipped cream, deodorant, spray paint, or other aerosol cans. They smoke dried banana peels, bay leaves, oregano, poppy seeds, rosemary, or dried tea leaves. They eat morning glory seeds. They boil nutmeg and drink the water. They smoke cigarettes with dried toothpaste. They sniff nail polish and remover. They spray insecticides on dried parsley and smoke it. And if that's not enough, they buy books on how to get high on the stuff in your house. Now...what was that about "if we could just stop the drug traffic"?

Previous anti-drug campaigns and scare tactics have resulted in increased usage of the drugs under attack. All the well intended publicity is free advertising and it creates consumers. It also informs kids of even more drugs than the ones they already know about. The media inadvertently promotes drugs with the detailed reports of drug effects. Both the effects and the risks may receive equal coverage, but kids remember the promise of excitement, not the dangerous consequences.

If you want to drug-proof kids, you must also deal with the fact that TV and movies show people having fun, using tobacco, alcohol, and drugs. Trying to convince children that these substances are not fun is no more likely to succeed than showing pictures of lung cancer will make people stop smoking. Kids at school will tell your kids how much fun it is. If the beginning stages of substance abuse weren't enjoyable, we would not have a drug problem.

Rather than continue with methods that have proven unsuccessful, these materials get at the root of the problem: poor self-concept, poor decision-making skills, lack of assertiveness, and the need for a handful of truthful facts. These materials, loaded with easy to do activities for all ages, will get you started in the right direction.

FIRST ACTIVITY FOR PARENTS

Just try saying "no" to coffee, tea, soda pop, and sugar (and tobacco and alcohol, if you use them) for a week. Keep a log of every time you break the "prohibition," what you were doing, how you were feeling, why you decided to do it anyway, and how you felt afterwards. Remember, all the reasons you have for breaking your abstinence are the same reasons kids use for taking drugs. The consequences are quite different, but the motives are very much the same.

Life Skills for
Drug Prevention

Self-Awareness and Drug Prevention

To be as sincerely happy as possible, it is important to be aware of, understand, and accept all of our feelings. Trying to act happy, when there are bad feelings lurking about, is not really happiness. It's camouflage. Pretending everything is OK, when it's not, is very common to beginning drug use.

Children must learn to own and understand their feelings before they can correct the cause of their unhappiness, anger, frustration, loneliness, feelings of inadequacy, despair, etc.

This self-awareness can begin with the physical self. Young children enjoy getting acquainted with themselves in a mirror. They like seeing their similarities and differences as compared to others. They may study their hands or elbows or noses or "toeses."

When young children get hurt and cry, we often say, "Oh, don't cry," or "Boys don't cry." This teaches them to deny their feelings, and be little hypocrites — acting differently than they honestly feel, to win your approval. When they get older and want to win peer approval, they won't listen to their own inner voice of what's right if they grew up squelching those feelings. If getting approval means using drugs, and approval is more important than feelings, what do you think they'll do?

By the time children are two or three, they have started learning about being mad, sad, frustrated, disappointed, scared, and other feelings they experience. The more they can feel safe to discuss these feelings, the less need they have to deny them.

Telling kids horror stories of children who have it worse, and "you should just quit feeling sorry for yourself and appreciate what you have," is not an effective means for growth. The fact that your arms and legs weren't cut off in an accident doesn't mean your own problems are things to be ignored, even if they're minor in comparison. While a paper cut, a stubbed toe, or a violated "funny bone" are not medical emergencies, these little problems need a few seconds of our total attention. Trying to pretend it never happened would take much more time and energy. This is even more true with emotions, which do not go away on their own. The more children's problems are discounted and/or repressed, the bigger they become.

It's unlikely you will find many people doing drugs who are comfortable and well acquainted with their feelings. It's usually the kid who angrily states, "I don't have any problems. I'm doin' OK," who is at risk for drug use. Everybody has reasons to feel sad, disappointed, angry, and discouraged at times. The child who does not show all of these feelings needs help.

ACTIVITIES FOR SELF-AWARENESS

1. Draw a group picture. You will need a box of crayons or markers and a big sheet of paper. The family is to draw a picture without talking.

   After 15-30 minutes (depending on the age of the kids and how things are going), have everyone stop. Then discuss how it felt to work together on a common project without being able to talk and plan. Discuss how everyone felt about their own part in the picture, as well as how they felt about their partners' actions. Did they learn anything about themselves, either from the activity or from others' comments afterward?

   This activity can show a lot about leadership, dominance, submission, confidence and a host of other qualities.

2. Take pictures of the bottoms of the children's feet. Have them lay down, with their pant legs pulled up, so there's nothing else

in the picture to give a clue to whose feet are whose. Keep track of the picture number for each child. When the pictures come back, see if the children know their own feet. Can you identify the feet that pitter-patter around your house?

3. Take a "trust walk." Kids get a partner and one is blind-folded. His partner takes him for a walk, trying to make it as safe and interesting as possible. After 10-15 minutes, reverse roles. Afterward, discuss how the children felt about their experience. What made it easy or hard to trust your partner? Did you learn anything about yourself or your partner?

4. Have a group hug. Everyone just forms a big huddle of people with their arms around each other. Discuss how it felt. Do it every day for a week or two, and then again discuss how it feels. Are there any patterns of who is always in the middle or outer edge? Is there anyone who would like to try it again from a different position? Has anyone noticed any changes in people since the first group hug?

5. Tell the kids to write an appreciation letter to someone. Make sure no one gets left out, even if you have to write a few letters yourself! Then write one to yourself. Afterwards, discuss which was easier to do, and what feelings the children had. Chances are, the majority of the children will have trouble writing appreciation to themselves.

6. Have the kid's shoes make up a story about what kind of person he is and what life is like as the shoes see it. "As My Shoes See Me" can include where kids go, what they do, how things look, all from a very different point of view.

7. Have each child write his full name vertically. By each letter, he will write something about himself that begins with that letter. It could be just a word or a sentence starting with the given letter. At the bottom of the paper, he can write anything else important that might not have fit by the letters of his name. If your child is too young or doesn't like to write, you can take dictation for him.

8. Ask the children to write descriptions of everyone in the family (using positive attributes!). Then read the descriptions and see if the kids can figure out who's who. Ask the children if they learned anything new about anyone.

9. Let children cut out pictures from magazines to make a "Me Collage." The pictures can show their interests and feelings. Encourage interaction between the kids so they can learn more about each other, and how each is both the same and different from everyone else.

10. Have the children use mirrors to draw a self-portrait.

11. Use a projector or other strong light to trace the shadow of each child's head on a colored paper. Cut out the silhouettes and paste them on another sheet of paper. The children can draw or cut-and-paste pictures to show what's on their mind. They can also write adjectives to describe themselves.

12. Let kids decorate their rooms, to reflect their values and interests.

13. Have the family members make a bag of things that tell who they are. Then everyone can share their bag and discuss why each thing is important.

14. Using a regular deck of cards, let kids play Rummy or Old Maid or some other easy game. Any time they discard or lay down cards, they must share a time they felt a certain way, based on the value of the cards. If all goes well, each time the kids play, they will spend more time discussing feelings and may even forget about the card game! Other words can be used to expand the game.

ace – happy	nine – embarrassed	five – discouraged
king – angry	eight – depressed	four – grateful
queen – scared	seven – excited	three – lucky
jack – confused	six – proud	two – hurt
ten – sad		

15. Make a feelings book. Each day give the kids a new word. Then they write in their book a time (or times) when they felt that way. Be sure the kids feel safe that others won't be seeing their books. Tell them whether you will or will not read their entries. Use the following list of feeling words on page 32.

16. Play charades, with kids acting out a feeling from the following list of feeling words on page 32.

17. Discuss what the kids want their lives to be like when they are grown up.

18. Make a collage of people's faces. Under each one, write how you think the person is feeling. Then make up a reason why he or she may be feeling that way.

19. Write a song or a poem about yourself.

20. Draw a floor plan or a picture of your room if it could be just the way you want it.

WHAT DO YOU BELIEVE?

Children need to explore what they believe, and under what rare conditions these beliefs should be flexible. They also need to practice making decisions based on their beliefs.

Designate one side of the room as *yes* and the other side as *no*. Read these questions and let the kids stand on the appropriate side of the room to show their opinion. They may want to stand in the middle of the room, but encourage them to make a choice. A *yes* answer doesn't always mean 100%: it can mean "more *yes* than *no*," or vice versa.

After the kids have made their decisions, you can also indicate your answer. Wait until they show their answer, so they have to do their own thinking.

This activity is not intended to teach "right" answers. These are just questions to help children understand what they believe.

Afterwards, discuss what the children learned or what they thought was interesting about this activity. Don't try to do all the questions in one day!

On another day, have children make up their own questions to use.

The questions can also be used for discussion topics, as long as no one is made to feel he has a "wrong opinion." Children will enjoy thinking of situations that could be "an exception to the rule." For example, you are not supposed to run a red light. But what if the intersection is empty, and there's an ambulance behind you with its lights and siren on? Or . . . you don't normally go outside naked. But what if you're in the tub and your house explodes in flames? Children need to understand their beliefs, and know there could be rare situations where it is necessary to be flexible.

1. Do you think kids should be able to pick out their own clothes?
2. Would you tell your friend if he had a hole in his pants?
3. Is it important to you to have a boyfriend or a girlfriend?
4. Will you be more strict with your children than your parents are with you?
5. Do you like going to church or attending religious services?
6. Should kids be allowed to watch all the TV they want?
7. Should kids do chores to earn their allowance?
8. Have you ever felt lonely?
9. Do you do more good things than bad things?
10. Is it easy for you to talk to your parents about important things?
11. Do you like to daydream?
12. Is religion important to you?
13. Do you like to spend a lot of time with your friends?
14. Do you enjoy spending some time alone?
15. Should we spend more money on the space program?
16. Should we spend more money on defense?
17. Would you like to be president?
18. Do you think mothers should stay home with their children?
19. Do you have enough friends?
20. Do you have enough money?
21. Do you have the things you really need the most?
22. Do you like to listen to music?
23. Do you like to read?
24. Do you like sports?

25. Do you think it's best to be an only child?
26. Do you like swimming?
27. Is it ever OK to cheat?
28. Do you have any secrets?
29. Can you tell your secrets to your best friends?
30. Should older brothers or sisters be the boss of the younger kids in a family?
31. Do you wish you were older?
32. Do you like to do things with your family?
33. Do you wish you lived somewhere else?
34. Should children be allowed to vote for the president?
35. When you're in a car, do you always wear seat belts?
36. Is it important for the adults in your life to understand you?
37. Do you like school?
38. Would you go to school if you didn't have to?
39. Do you like to give people presents?
40. Would you like to try parachuting?
41. Do you like eating with your family?
42. Have you ever stolen anything, even something little like a pen or pair of scissors from school?
43. Do you like to sleep?
44. Should people get welfare checks without having to do any work?
45. Would the world be better if the kids were in charge?
46. Should kids be able to do what ever they want?
47. Have you ever wished you had different parents?
48. Have you ever wished you had a different teacher?
49. Would you like to own a boat?
50. Would you like to go to the moon?
51. Are you happy?
52. Should drugs be legal?
53. If you knew someone who sold drugs, would you turn them in?
54. Would you like to be in a play?
55. Do you save some of your money?
56. Do you like to make presents for people?
57. Do you like animals?
58. Do you like little kids?
59. Is it easy to admit when you do something wrong?

60. Are your feelings hurt easily?
61. Do you get mad a lot?
62. Does it show when you're mad?
63. Have you ever felt left out?
64. Would you go to the dentist and doctor if your parents didn't make you?
65. Are good grades important to you?
66. Do you want your children to have the same beliefs about religion that your parents do?
67. Would you take a job you hated if it paid a lot of money?
68. Do you like to sit and think?
69. Do you like to be in the country and look at nature?
70. Should kids smoke?
71. Should adults smoke?
72. Do you wish there were more kids in your family?
73. Would you marry someone who has a different religion?
74. Do you like knowing people of different races?
75. Would you like to dye your hair another color?
76. Should people pierce their ears?
77. Do you want to go to college?
78. Do you ever watch educational TV?
79. Will you spank your children?
80. Do you like to have your friends meet your parents?
81. Would you like to be famous?
82. Would you like to be rich?
83. Have you ever wished you were younger?
84. Would you try a marijuana cigarette if your friend wanted you to?
85. Do you like classical music?
86. Would you like to be in the military some day?
87. Do you like to answer the phone?
88. Would you like to ride a motorcycle?
89. Do you like to participate in class?
90. Do you like doing this?
91. Do you think you will keep the same beliefs as your parents?
92. Would you like a TV in your bedroom?
93. At home, do you spend most of your time in your room?
94. Would you like to live in another country?
95. Would you like to go to an all-boys or all-girls school?

96. Do you think drugs can be bad for people?
97. Should kids have pets?
98. Would you like to live in the country?
99. Do you like to eat breakfast?
100. Do you wish you could stay up later?
101. Do you watch TV every day?
102. Do you like to travel?
103. Will you smoke someday?
104. Will you ever try drugs?
105. Do you think people just decide to be alcoholics or drug addicts?
106. Do you like to go to a lot of movies?
107. Do you like to be teased in a fun way?
108. Would you like to go to Disney World?
109. Do you like to watch cartoons?
110. Do you want to have kids when you are an adult?
111. Do you think it is OK for little girls to play with cars and trucks?
112. Do you think it is OK for little boys to play with dolls?
113. Should kids be paddled at school?
114. Do you like to go shopping?
115. Would you rather be another color?
116. Should we give more money to the poor?
117. Does it matter if the air is dirty?
118. Have you ever lied to your friends?
119. Have you lied today during this activity?
120. Do you like snow?
121. Would you like a snake for a pet?
122. When you get married, is it important that the person be good-looking?
123. Would you tell your friend if he or she smelled bad?
124. Are your grades more important to your parents than they are to you?
125. Do you like homework?
126. Do you wish you looked better?
127. Do you ever wish you were someone else?
128. When your parents are old, will you want them to live with you?

129. If you bought a friend a gift and he didn't like it, would you want him to tell you?
130. Is it ever right to kill?
131. If you were suddenly rich, would you share your money?
132. Do you eat a lot of junk food?
133. Do you take vitamins?
134. Do you like doing arts and crafts?
135. Do you like working on cars?
136. Do you like cleaning house?
137. Have you ever shot a gun?
138. Would you like to be a surgeon?
139. Do some kids at school need to behave better?
140. Do you like history?
141. Would you like to be a teacher?
142. Do you have someone who can help you with your homework?
143. Do you like to watch sunsets?
144. Do you want your friends to tell you what they really think and feel?
145. Do you like jokes?
146. Do you like to sleep late?
147. Should kids go to school in the summer and have a short vacation every month or two?
148. Should adults have to take classes in how to be good parents?
149. Is it important to have some quiet time?
150. This is the last question. Would you like to do more another day?

"A BOOK ABOUT ME"

Kids can make a book, *All about Me*. Staple 20 sheets of paper with a construction paper cover. Kids can decorate the cover. Every day assign one of the topics. The kids can copy it, write their answers, and illustrate it. If you are a teacher, this gives you high quality seatwork with little of your time consumed.

Most of the topics are written in the plural form so children don't feel they have to have only one favorite and everything else is second best. (For example, with today's split homes and remarriages, it's important that children don't feel they have to pick one favorite parent, that it's OK to love them all equally.)

1. These are my favorite things to do.
2. These are my favorite people.
3. These are my favorite stories.
4. These are my favorite toys.
5. These are my favorite TV shows.
6. I'm really happy when...
7. I'm really mad when...
8. I wish everyone would...
9. At school I'm best at...
10. At school I'm not good at...
11. When I grow up...
12. I'm good at...
13. My teacher thinks I'm...
14. I need help with...
15. My favorite animals are...
16. I wish I...
17. I'm glad I learned...
18. If I ran the school...
19. If I were the boss at home...
20. The most important things I know are...

RECOMMENDED READING

T.A. for Tots and Other Prinzes; Alvyn M. Freed; Jalmar Press, Inc.; Sacramento, California; 1974

Values; William Hendricks; Educational Service, Inc.; Stevensville, Michigan; 1984

Values Clarification; Sidney B. Simon, Leland W. Howe, & Howard Kirschenbaum; Hart Publishing Company; New York; 1972

FEELING WORDS

affectionate	hurt	restless
angry	hysterical	righteous
annoyed	ignored	sad
apprehensive	impressed	safe
bad	inadequate	satisfied
bored	intimidated	scared
brave	isolated	secured
calm	jealous	shocked
cheated	jumpy	silly
cocky	kind	skeptical
competitive	lazy	smart
confused	left out	sneaky
destructive	lonely	solemn
determined	loving	sorry
dread	mean	spiteful
embarrassed	miserable	startled
empty	naughty	stingy
energetic	nervous	strange
excited	nutty	stupid
exhausted	obnoxious	sure
fascinated	obsessed	suspicious
foolish	outrage	sympathetic
fortunate	overwhelmed	talkative
frustrated	panic	tempted
furious	peaceful	tense
good	persecuted	terrible
greedy	petrified	terrified
grouchy	pity	threatened
guilty	pressured	tired
gullible	proud	trapped
happy	puzzled	troubled
hate	quarrelsome	uneasy
helpful	rage	upset
helpless	rejected	violent
homesick	relaxed	vulnerable
honored	relieved	wonderful
horrible	remorse	worried

Self-Esteem
and Drugs

Children who like themselves do better in school. And kids who do better in school are most able to say no to drugs. They get lots of approval. They don't need to desperately seek approval from someone, anyone. They have SELF-approval. Peer pressure tactics of belittling them, or threatening to dislike them, are not as powerful to children who like themselves.

The best way to help children like themselves is for the adults in their lives to truly like them. Treat them with the respect you would give an adult you liked.

Our everyday comments to children teach them how to feel about themselves. When the baseball goes through the living room window, shouting "You're so stupid!" will not fix the window and will damage self-worth. "What did you just learn?" and discussing ways to pay for the damage will be more productive and will leave the self-esteem intact. *If you wouldn't say it "that way" to your boss, maybe you could find a kinder way to say it to your child.*

Self-esteem changes, but it does take time. And the older the child, the longer it takes. So don't give up just because you don't get tremendous improvement immediately. It may take months, or years to rebuild poor self-esteem.

WAYS TO BUILD SELF-ESTEEM:

1. Make three times as many positive comments as suggestions for improvement.

2. Give several honest compliments every day. If you get desperate, you can always say "Your eyes are just the right distance apart." Seriously, every child does a few things right. It can be as simple as "I appreciate your getting to school on time every morning." If you must compare children, do so in a positive manner, comparing them with generic others outside the home or class. For example, "Some kids are so noisy. I really appreciate how quiet you are."

3. Have children keep a diary of self-strokes. Every day they write in something they did well. They can also write in compliments they received from others. On bad days, they'll have something encouraging to read.

4. Be encouraging to children when they are having difficulties. Saying "That's easy — if you had a brain in your head, you wouldn't be having so much trouble," is not going to build confidence. Instead, be supportive — "I remember when I studied that in math. I thought I'd never get it. Let's work on it together. After awhile, you'll catch on. Sometimes it takes awhile, but that's OK."

5. Listen to kids and their ideas. If you tell them they'll never accomplish their crazy dreams, they probably won't. If they believe in themselves, they will accomplish a great deal more. Maturity assesses dreams for reality much better than does criticism.

6. Deal with problems in a positive manner. Children need to know that mistakes are ways to learn. Discussing what they can do differently next time is much more productive than yelling insults.

ACTIVITIES TO BUILD SELF-ESTEEM

1. Give everyone self-sticking labels. Have them write a compliment for each member of the family. Then everyone sticks the label on each person, and tells them the compliment. Encourage eye contact and use of the person's name.

2. Once a week, ask for a volunteer to be "it." Then each member of the family takes turns giving compliments to that person, whose only response is "thank you."

   Encourage diversity of comments, so no one hears a meaningless "You're nice" from everyone.

   After everyone has said all they want, it is interesting to ask the person who was "it" how he feels. Often, he'll be surprised that there were so many good things said. And what a nice surprise it is!

3. Have everyone write a commercial or make a poster promoting themselves.

4. Have the kids fold a paper so there are 12-16 squares when it is unfolded. Then have the kids collect autographs and positive comments from everyone in the family. Make one for yourself, too! If you have colored felt tip pens for everyone to use, this will make the finished paper look nice and feel more special.

5. Have the children write down every negative thing that is said to them (including what they say or think to themselves!) in one day. Then have them write down if they think the criticism was valid, and if so, whether they want to do anything about it or not.

   First, they must decide if it is something they can change, like sloppy work. If someone calls them "shorty," then they need to accept that they can't change their height, and learn to not internalize rude comments (a very difficult job!).

   If the criticism reflects something they can change, then they need to decide if they want to change. A child may not want to wear a style he doesn't like, just to please others. If he does want to change, then he needs to think about how he will do that. The point is — children need to learn to evaluate the validity of every criticism, and that they don't have to please everyone all the time.

This activity can help children develop realistic pictures of themselves. They need to own both the positive and negative aspects about themselves, and know in what areas they want to change and in what ways they want to stay the same (at least for now).

6. Put a large mirror in a box. Cover it with a curtain or towel. Put a sign above the box that says "The Most Important Thing in Your Life." Discuss what might be in the box, and then let the kids, one at a time, take a look. Tell them not to say what they see. After everyone has looked in the box, discuss how they are the most important thing in their own life. (Parents and teachers can try to help them, but they make the decisions that affect their lives. As they get older, they become totally responsible for their own lives. No one can make the right choices for them.)

7. Make a compliment bag. Each day, everyone writes down something good they have seen someone else do. The compliment is put in the bag. Throughout the week, pull out a few compliments and read them aloud. Then give the paper to the person who was complimented, or keep them to put in a scrap book.

This activity can be kept going for as long as there is interest.

8. Have the kids write a list of things they wish someone would tell them (for example, "I'm polite, I'm smart, I'm cute, I'm a good kid," etc.). Collect the lists.

Several days later, have each child make a certificate for himself. Collect the certificates, but don't tell them what you are going to do with them.

Write on their certificates everything they wanted to hear, as long as you believe it is true. If it isn't find a way to make a positive statement about that quality. If a child wants to be told "I'm nice" and he's a big bully, you can write, "You want to be nice." Or, "You were nice when you shared the ball yesterday." That way, you are reinforcing his good desires, without saying something he knows isn't really true.

For the kids who have a short list, add a few of your own that you think would be meaningful.

9. Have the kids list everything that's good about them and the good things they have done. It can be about school, friends, sports, talents, behavior, attitude, appearance...anything and everything!

RECOMMENDED READING

Your Child's Self-Esteem; Dorothy Corkille Briggs; Doubleday & Company, Inc.; Garden City, NY; 1975

100 Ways to Enhance Self-Concept in the Classroom: A Handbook for Parents and Teachers; Jack Canfield & Harold C. Wells; Prentice-Hall, Inc.; Englewood Cliffs, NJ 1976

Project Self-Esteem: A Parent Involvement Program for Elementary Age Children; Sandy McDaniel & Peggy Beelen; B.L. Winch & Associates; Rolling Hills Estates, CA; 1986

Thinking Skills and Drugs

To "say no" to drugs, a child must be able to evaluate the offer and make a logical decision. This skill is used not only to say no to drugs, but in every aspect of life. Although some decisions are easy and do not require much analysis, this is not always the case. Kids must be taught critical thinking skills so they can evaluate the data, weigh the choices, and decide what is really best for them.

Children must be able to evaluate their own beliefs, as well as the beliefs of others. As children get older, they *will* make decisions for themselves. We have no control over that. Our only choice is whether we will provide the necessary skills for them to make their decisions intelligently.

Kids will hear all kinds of good things about drugs from the other kids at school. You have no control over that. Trying to teach children "just say no" will not be very effective unless we teach good thinking skills first. Kids must learn that sometimes they need more information before making a decision. It's OK to say "I don't know," or "I don't want to right now," and then get more information from a legitimate source.

Another important skill is separating logical and emotional thinking, knowing when each is appropriate, and keeping a balance in life. No one wants a child to give up a hobby because it's not a

38

logical need, nor a child who has fun watching TV all night and never studies.

Kids need to keep their questioning minds. Little children are always asking "why?" If all they hear is "Because I said so," or "You ask too many questions," they may believe you. And then when someone wants them to try drugs, they may do it without question.

It is important for children to learn the difference between fact and opinion, and the difference between what *is* true and what *might* be true. This will help them sort out everything they hear about drugs. They need to do their own thinking instead of blindly following every thing that comes their way.

Kids need to be aware that words mean slightly different things to different people. (Like when you tell a child who is going to get a shot, "It won't hurt much"!) Along with this, it is important for them to learn to be careful of generalizations and statements with absolutes, such as *all, none, always,* and *never.* When other kids are trying to talk them into something, their words are seldom literally true. Children need to be able to sort through the persuasion of drug-using peers.

All of these skills can be developed through discussions, research, projects, etc., which require more than just memorizing details. Children need to develop higher levels of comprehension: application, analysis, synthesis, and evaluation. They must be able to understand and interpret what they see, hear, think, and read, so they can apply what they learn to new situations when you aren't there to help. Kids can break information down into parts to be analyzed, looking for assumptions, opinions, and other errors in reasoning. They can learn to integrate their knowledge so they can put together a new idea, concept, or theory. These skills will enable children to evaluate information and allow them to make more logical, productive decisions.

With today's wide range of choices, kids who don't use critical thinking skills will be seriously handicapped in their decision making. And what affects their lives more than their decisions? With the constant input of information from every imaginable source, today's kids must be skilled in correctly evaluating what they see, hear, think, and read. Only then can they make the best possible decisions in their lives.

A GOOD THINKER...

1. is open to new ideas.

2. does not argue when he knows nothing about the subject.

3. knows when he needs more information.

4. knows the difference between what might be true and what *is* true.

5. knows that people have different ideas about the meanings of words.

6. avoids common mistakes in his own reasoning.

7. questions things that don't make sense to him.

8. separates emotional thinking from logical thinking and knows when each is appropriate.

9. builds his vocabulary so he can understand others and can explain his own ideas better.

10. knows it's silly to argue about a fact that is available as public record.

11. knows the difference between fact and opinion—and does not argue about opinions.

12. knows he makes mistakes and evaluates his own thoughts.

ACTIVITIES TO DEVELOP CRITICAL THINKING

1. Have children cut out an ad for a product they would like to buy. Discuss all the things they would need to find out before deciding whether that's how they want to spend their money.

2. Have the children find two ads of different brands or models of something they want to buy. Then discuss and list the questions they would need answered to make the best choice.

3. Talk about the following topics. Some of the suggested questions are about grown-up subjects, but little kids love these questions best — not being in the situation, they have all the answers! What things do you need to find out before:

A. joining a ball team
B. leaving on vacation with your family
C. buying a gift for someone
D. buying a new bike or stereo
E. going to a movie
F. taking a job
G. going out on a date with someone
H. getting married
I. deciding whether to go to college, and if so, where
J. picking a house or apartment to live in

FACT OR OPINION?

Discuss whether each statement is a fact or opinion. Remember, facts can be proved. Opinions do not need to be proved and everyone can have a different opinion. Facts are true statements that everyone will agree with and opinions are the different things people like, think, or believe. It is not the same thing as true and false. It's not a fact just because you agree with it! Example:

A. Cats are better than dogs. (opinion)
B. Dogs normally have four legs. (fact)

1. Astronauts have gone to the moon. (fact)
2. The space program is very important. (opinion)
3. Kids should have a big allowance. (opinion)
4. Chocolate ice cream is best. (opinion)
5. Red is the prettiest color. (opinion)
6. All kids need to breathe. (fact)
7. People should be allowed to drive as fast as they want. (opinion)

8. If you drive too fast, you might get a speeding ticket. (fact)
9. Cats should wear a bell to warn the birds. (opinion)
10. Kids like pizza best. (opinion)
11. Women should have careers, like men do. (opinion)
12. Mothers should stay home with their children and not have other jobs. (opinion)
13. Hamburgers taste better than liver. (opinion)
14. Poison is not good for you. (fact)
15. Drugs kill some people. (fact)
16. Kids play their music too loudly. (opinion)
17. Kids talk on the phone too much. (opinion)
18. Babies are cute. (opinion)
19. It costs money to raise kids. (fact)
20. Adults should vote in elections. (opinion)
21. Fish live in water. (fact)
22. Everyone needs to learn how to use computers. (opinion)
23. If you're careful, drugs won't hurt you. (opinion)
24. School is not important. (opinion)
25. People need food or nourishment to stay alive. (fact)
26. Cars need fuel to run. (fact)
27. Kids listened to better music 20-30 years ago. (opinion)
28. Young girls shouldn't wear make-up. (opinion)
29. Girls shouldn't call boys on the telephone. (opinion)
30. It's usually safer to wear seat belts. (fact)
31. We need stricter gun control. (opinion)
32. Everyone should be allowed to own a gun. (opinion)
33. Some people use guns to shoot other people. (fact)
34. All the old black and white movies should be colorized. (opinion)
35. The old black and white movies are art and shouldn't be colorized. (opinion)
36. People watch too much TV. (opinion)
37. Some people think that people watch too much TV. (fact)
38. Most people watch TV everyday. (fact)
39. Video games are a waste of money. (opinion)
40. Kids are a lot smarter than they used to be. (opinion)

If the kids liked this activity, they can use their ideas to make more examples.

ABSOLUTES

These statements have absolute words like *all, none, always, never,* etc. Discuss whether each statement is *true* or *false.* Think carefully, because they are tricky! Very few statements with absolutes are true statements.

For each false statement, discuss ways to change it so it will be true.

1. All living people breathe. (true)

2. Everyone else has a nice stereo. (probably false — who do you know that doesn't?)

3. All the other kids have pets. (Can you name one kid in the whole world that doesn't have a pet?)

4. No one likes a murderer. (probably false. Every time a murderer is on trial, some one defends him and shows they care. Even if the person is convicted, even if the person admits he is guilty, there always seems to be someone who claims undying love for this person.)

5. All people normally have two arms. (true)

6. Everyone gets a bigger allowance than I do. (probably false. Take a survey of every kid in the world, or at least of every kid in your school, and see if it's true.)

7. You should never hurt anyone. (false. How can the nurse give you a shot without hurting you? What if someone is trying to kidnap you?)

8. Teachers never make mistakes. (false)

9. All animals need food to live. (true)

10. School is never fun. (false. Ask if anyone ever had any fun at school.)

11. Everyone loves Christmas. (false. Christmas is very depressing for some people who are sad, lonely, or poor. And some people don't celebrate Christmas.)

12. I never get a turn. (probably false. Can anyone remember you ever having a turn at something?)

13. Boys are taller than girls. (false. No absolute words are used, but all is implied. It's easy to find exceptions to generalities.)

14. Parents never get any appreciation. (false. Has anyone ever showed some appreciation to their parents?)

15. All the teachers are rotten. (false)

16. All cars need fuel, or some form of energy, to run. (true)

17. You should always do what you're told. (false. What if a stranger tells you to get in his car, or someone tells you to steal for them?)

18. Older people know best. (false. What if they're giving you drugs?)

19. No one cares about me anyway. (probably false. Even kids abandoned by their parents are taken care of by a stranger who cares. If you have lots of problems, you may have trouble finding people who will care, and keep caring, but there are some out there if you look hard enough.)

20. You always treat me like a baby. (false. Are you wearing diapers and drinking a bottle? At least you are being treated as an adult with your food and clothes.)

21. I can't ever say no. (false. Do you want to take a test on advanced nuclear physics or drink cod liver oil? I bet you can say no to that.)

22. You should always be polite. (false. Even if you're being kidnapped?)

23. You should never tell on anyone. (false. Even if someone's hurting or bothering you and says not to tell?)

24. It's always wrong to kill animals. (false. What if one is suffering and has no hope of recovering?)

25. All the world has gone crazy. (false. It just seems that way.)

APPLICATION

Pick out a proverb or axiom, or think of one of your own. Tell what it means and think of five different situations to apply the rule.

Honey attracts more flies than vinegar.
A stitch in time saves nine.
A penny saved is a penny earned.
All good things must come to an end.
Where there's smoke, there's fire.
Birds of a feather flock together.
Every cloud has a silver lining.
You can't judge a book by its cover.
Easy come, easy go.
Better late than never.
Beauty is only skin deep.
Too many chiefs and not enough Indians.
Too many cooks spoil the broth.
A watched pot never boils.

Make up your own proverb and draw a picture to show what it means. It can be something silly, like "It's easier to find milk than donuts."

MIGHT BE TRUE VS. IS DEFINITELY TRUE

Discuss each sentence. Decide if it might be true or if it is definitely true. Think carefully! These can be tricky!

1. It gets dark outside at night. (might be true. Not in northern Canada and Alaska in the summer, so it depends where you are.)

2. My car's gone — someone stole my car! (might be true. Or you forgot where you parked it.)

3. People can suffocate inside a plastic bag. (must be true.)

4. Nobody could have survived that crash. (might be true. There are often people who survive against incredible odds — and have been left for dead because of this dangerous assumption!)

5. There is snow on the ground, so the temperature is less than 32 degrees Fahrenheit. (might be true. The snow is 32 degrees or less, but the air temperature could be warmer.)

6. That boy is in a bad mood almost all the time lately. He must be on drugs. (might be true. Maybe he has other problems.)

7. The Earth is a planet. (must be true.)

8. That girl speaks a foreign language. She must be from another country. (might be true. Lots of native-born Americans speak other languages.)

9. We have the best team, so we will win the game. (might be true. You wish!)

10. The baby is crying. He must be hungry. (might be true. He might be tired, or wet, or sick, or mad, or...)

11. Hardly anyone ordered a school lunch today. The menu must be terrible. (might be true. Maybe there's something else going on and the kids will be gone at lunch time.)

12. Everyone in this class has a good report card. The teacher must be grading too easy. (might be true. Or maybe everyone is smart and working hard.)

13. You have a bad grade on this test. You must not have studied. (might be true. Or maybe you didn't understand what you studied, or the test was too hard.)

14. Fresh water freezes at 32 degrees Fahrenheit. (must be true.)

15. That little kid is always dirty. His parents must not care about him. (might be true. Maybe they don't have running water, maybe he just likes to get dirty first thing every day, or maybe they care a lot about him but don't think being clean is important.)

16. You must have done something wrong or you wouldn't have been fired. (might be true. On rare occasions, people are fired with no valid reason.)

17. That's the smoke alarm! The house is on fire! (might be true. Maybe someone burned the toast again.)

18. Did you hear that? There must be a burglar in the house! (might be true. Maybe the dog is sleep walking again.)

19. I don't have to do my homework. It's snowing really hard. The schools will be closed tomorrow. (might be true. Sometimes schools are open even when they shouldn't be.)

20. If you don't like the weather, be patient and it will change. (must be true — It may take a week, but the weather always changes eventually.)

SEMANTICS

Find out how people's ideas differ about the same words. Pick a question and interview people. Find out their ideas on the underlined words. Talk to people outside your family, too. That will give you a greater variety of answers.

1. What is *fun* for you?
2. What *tastes good* to you?
3. What is *relaxing* for you?
4. What is *boring* for you?
5. What is *scary* to you?
6. What temperature feels *hot* or *cold* to you?
7. What does a *good* person do?

LOGICAL OR EMOTIONAL THINKING

Read each sentence and decide if it is logical or emotional. Logical statements are based on facts. Emotional statements use words that arouse feelings, express an opinion based on emotion, and often exaggerate by use of generalities or absolutes.

If Mr. Spock wouldn't say it, it's an emotional statement. Remember, this is not a judgment of good or bad. Each kind of thinking is appropriate under certain conditions.

1. People are killing a lot of whales. (logical)

2. This is terrible! Soon there will be no whales left! (*Terrible* is an emotional term.)

3. Drunk drivers kill a lot of people in car accidents. (logical)

4. It's an outrage that people drive when they are drunk. They should all be shot. (*Outrage* is an emotional word. The proposed solution is based on feelings.)

5. The purpose of schools is to teach people what they need to know. (logical)

6. Schools do not teach everyone the skills they need. (logical)

7. Some people think the school system needs a lot of changes. (logical)

8. School is just a waste of time. (Exaggeration, generality, emotional)

9. It's just awful the way young people are these days. (*Awful* is an emotional word, and the statement is a generality.)

10. Some people don't approve of the behavior of most young people. (logical)

11. It's 483 miles to go until we are home. (logical)

12. We still have 483 more miles. We'll never get home! (Emotional—exaggeration, *never* is an absolute and probably not true in this case.)

13. Americans consume 60% of the world's illegal drugs. Drugs are a bigger problem here than in any other country. (logical)

14. It's just a crime the way parents don't control their children anymore. (*Crime* is an emotional word, and the statement is an absolute that doesn't apply to everyone.)

15. This country is on the road to ruin. Too many people are just doing whatever they want. (Emotional, generalization)

RECOMMENDED READING

Critical Thinking (book 1 & 2); Anita Harnadek; Midwest Publications; Pacific Grove, CA; 1976

Persuasive Tactics

There are many techniques used to influence people's choices and decisions. The more kids are aware of these subtle tactics, the better their chances of making independent, logical decisions.

THE BANDWAGON

Kids use this all the time. This argument gives the impression that you'll be left out if you don't (whatever), because everyone else is.

"But, Mom, everyone else is doing it." Or "Nobody does that anymore. Were you born in the Dark Ages?"

"Hey, Don, everyone's having a cigarette. You gotta try one, too."

NAME-CALLING

Another popular one, name-calling uses emotional words to get an emotional response, instead of a logical one.

"You're a sissy if you don't. What are you, chicken? This beer's not going to hurt you. You know that."

"What an old-fashioned prude!"

And it can be used as a complimentary manipulative as well.

"You're such a good friend. I know you'll hide these drugs for me."

REPETITION

This skill is mastered by the age of two. Repeating the same thing over and over, the idea becomes deeply embedded in your brain.

"Can I? Can I? Can I? Huh, can I?"

"Can I borrow the car Friday night?" asked every week even though you say "no" every week.

"This drug's really great. You gotta try it. It's really great. I know you'll like it. It's just the greatest!"

INNUENDO

This one comes a little later in childhood. Something is implied without anyone coming right out and saying it.

"My lemonade costs more because the cat didn't fall in mine." Well, the cat didn't fall in the competitor's lemonade either — it's just falsely implied, although not directly stated.

"Kris's mom is so understanding. She lets Kris wear make up to school every day now."

"Greg's parents buy him beer for his parties because they trust him."

TRANSFER

This one is a bit trickier. It involves arousing some feelings about a person or situation, and then transferring them to a different person or situation. It can be done with positive or negative feelings.

> "Tom has lots of girlfriends, and he has a mustache. I think I'll grow one, too."

> "Remember how mad you got at Uncle Wes at the reunion last year? And it was so crowded. Let's use our vacation to go to the beach. You can just relax and have some peace and quiet for a change."

> "Lyn's got so many friends. Maybe if I party with her, I can make some friends, too."

GENERALIZING

A lot of description is used, with no facts.

> "This is the best stereo. It looks good. It plays great and it'll last forever. And it's cheap. Mom, I've just got to have it."

Notice, no facts are given. Better than what? Cheaper than what? What will happen if he doesn't get it?

> "Suzy knows everything a good class president needs to know. She has lots of good ideas to make this a better school."

What does a good class president need to know? What are these ideas that are supposed to be "good"? Lots of promises, no information.

> "Drugs are really cool. Everybody's doing it, and we're all having a good time. It's really great to get high."

TESTIMONIAL

A "famous" person is quoted. And, of course, you will agree — or so it is hoped.

"But Andrea said I should buy these jeans, and she's the smartest girl in the class."

"My favorite rock star does drugs, and his songs say how great it is."

BARGAIN OR FREE

A very popular tactic, giving you something for nothing, or for a fraction of what you think it's worth.

"But, Dad, it's free! All we have to do is send in 486 box tops by next month."

"The tapes are on sale, two for one. I've just got to get some while they're so cheap! Please give me next month's allowance."

"Here, try this stuff. You're new, so it's free."

A deadline is given, or there is a limited supply, and surely you don't want to miss out!

"I've got to have this form signed today, and the bus is going to be here — hurry!"

"Our class only needs 89 more cans to win the canned food drive, and tomorrow's the last day. How many can you give me?"

"I can get this bike half price, but the sale ends this weekend."

"Come on, have a drink with us. What are you waiting for?"

THE COMMON PEOPLE

"You're just a regular guy like me, so of course, you'll agree with me. We common people gotta stick together." This argument is not usually used by children, but you will see it in advertising.

> "I'm a working man, just like you. We work hard and we deserve a good product when we buy."

> "I'm a mother of two young children, and I have a career, too. I don't have time for a headache, do you? This is the brand I use."

> "You want a good, cold beer," and the ad shows men watching the football game on TV.

YUPPIE APPEAL

You're a cut above the average if you are able to truly appreciate this quality product, if you won't settle for anything but the very best.

> "Mom, I need $50 for your present, because I want to buy you the very best."

> "But, Dad, this one is so much better, and it'll last longer. You don't want to get me that junky one. Lisa's dad bought her the top of the line, and I'd be embarrassed to show her this crummy thing."

> "You work hard in school, and you've got lots of bucks. You can afford to have a good time — try this stuff."

AVOIDING THE SUBJECT

The person either subtly changes the subject, or distracts you by arguing a minor point.

You ask your child if his homework is done, and he says, "Mom, have you seen this documentary? It's all about..."

"I know you don't like me spending time with Alice, but remember, you didn't like Kim either, and she hasn't gotten into any trouble at all. You were wrong, Mom."

"You said I couldn't watch that movie at Bob's house. But I didn't go to Bob's house, I was at Ken's."

"Ah, don't be worried about all that bad stuff you hear. Try this. I do it all the time, and I'm OK. No problem."

MODERNISM

This is a new idea, so it has to be better.

"This is the 20th century. Get with it. This is the style now."

"Look at the world you gave us. It's for sure your ways didn't work, so don't knock the new ways."

"This is the latest stuff out, and is it great!"

OLD FASHIONEDISM

This is the way it's always been done. Don't give up the old traditions for these silly new ideas.

"We've done it this way since the dawn of time. If man were meant to..., he'd have been born with..."

"Sure there's problems, but there's no need to throw the baby out with the bath water. There's nothing wrong with the old ways, there's just a few little problems to straighten out."

"People have been drinking ever since they left the caves. If it were so bad, people would've all died out a million years ago. We don't need drugs, we'll just drink our beer."

PERSONAL ATTACK

Instead of addressing the issue, the person is attacked and discredited.

"Don't tell me I don't know the right thing to do. You've been seeing a shrink for years, so who are you to judge?"

"You just don't want to share your new car with me, that's all. If you weren't so selfish, there wouldn't be a problem with me using it Saturday night."

"You're just a nerd. Everybody does this stuff. It's no big deal. You're just afraid to try anything."

EMOTIONAL REACTION

Emotional terms are used to get you feeling, rather than thinking. They may try to make you feel angry, prejudiced, sympathetic, or patriotic. They may ridicule, bring up the issue of fairness, call names, flatter you, or appeal to your sense of morals or generosity.

"Mom, it'll just ruin my life if you ground me and I miss the big game."

"It's not fair. It's just not fair."

"You're such a great dad, I just know you'll go along with my idea."

"This dress was made for you. It'll be perfect for the dance. It's the perfect shade of blue, and it makes your eyes look so bright. You look absolutely lovely in it."

"You're not going to believe this, Dad. This dumb teacher won't approve me to play in Friday's game just because I didn't turn in one little homework assignment. This game's really important, and I've gotta play. Lots of kids don't do every single homework assignment. You've gotta do something, Dad."

"What a wimp. You're such a nerd. I can't believe you're too chicken to try this stuff."

IT COULD BE WORSE

A worse condition is named, in hopes you'll be more accepting of the current situation.

"It's only a D. Lots of people get D's, and even F's."

"I know I've got D's and F's on my report card, but at least I go to classes. Lots of kids cut all the time."

"Yes, I'm an hour late getting home. I suppose you'd be happier if I'd had a car wreck and was dead—at least then I'd have a reason and you wouldn't be all bent out of shape."

"It's only a cigarette. It's not like you're doing drugs or anything like that."

QUOTING AUTHORITY

A recognized authority figure is quoted, and the assumption is made that the authority couldn't possibly be wrong.

"But my teacher said to do it this way. That's how we do math now."

"As president of student council, I know what needs to be done. I don't need a committee to tell me how to do my job."

"My favorite football player eats this cereal, so it's got to be good."

"Your favorite sports star does this stuff all the time, and he's going great."

ACTIVITIES TO EVALUATE PERSUASION TACTICS

1. Make a notebook, collecting advertisements for each example of persuasive techniques.

2. Each family member reads an advertisement. Discuss which techniques have been used. (There are often several in a single ad.)

3. Design an ad for each category of persuasive techniques.

4. Write and act out a TV commercial to illustrate these techniques.

5. Watch TV commercials and analyze their persuasive contents.

6. Discuss how these persuasive tactics are used by friends to talk you into things, whether harmless — like whether to go to the game, or serious — like cigarettes, alcohol, and/or drugs.

7. Pretend you are a door-to-door salesman. Pick a product you want to sell, and plan the speech you will use. Then act it out, with someone else being the potential customer. Discuss whether the prospect would have bought the product, and their reasons for buying or for keeping their money.

8. Read examples of the persuasion tactics and see how many the family can identify.

9. Discuss all the ways people (friends, family, teachers, etc.) try to persuade you.

Discipline, Peer Pressure, and Assertiveness: How To Say No To Drugs

How we discipline kids is the first determining factor in how they deal with peer pressure. If you give them positive comments in the form of "I like how you...", the child learns to please you. His sense of importance and self-worth is tied to what you think.

This works very nicely until the child is seven or eight. Then it becomes more important to please his peers. If his peers think drugs are cool, guess what he will do to feel important. A kid has no ability to withstand peer pressure if he has spent his whole life learning to feel good by pleasing those people most important to them.

Only a minor change in our comments is needed. Instead of "You're such a good boy when you clean your room," or "I like it when you help set the table," just shift the comment from the person to the behavior and the consequence. Leave out the part of how it pleases you or makes them good. "Your room looks really nice now. You did a good job cleaning it." "I see you set the table. It helps a lot when I don't have to get everything ready by myself." These comments still recognize and reinforce the child's good behavior, but the focus is on the job and/or his contribution — not his self-worth or value to you.

Actively teaching assertiveness and resistance to negative peer pressure (if kids have the "right" peers, the pressure is positive) can be started with three year olds. Since these qualities are very natural in a two year old, all we need to do is maintain them and add a few social graces.

Children need to know they don't always have to please other children. Sometimes they will want to make their own decisions. And they will learn that instead of a tantrum or a bonk on the head, "No, thank you," or "I don't want to right now," is more appropriate.

It helps if there are areas where kids don't have to please you at all, such as, toy selection or choice of ice cream. Comments like, "Oh, don't buy that puzzle, it won't be any fun. Get this one," teaches kids to let others make their decisions. After all, if he isn't "smart enough" to make even a minor choice like that, he certainly won't feel competent to handle a big choice like cigarettes, alcohol, or drugs. He'll just let his friends decide, like he used to let his parents decide.

Teach kids to use "I messages," where they state how they feel and why. This is a valuable communication skill and is helpful in being assertive and in dealing with negative peer pressure. They can practice this skill at home with the family and at school with other kids.

Unfortunately, not everyone is comfortable with a child who says, "I feel mad because I don't think you're being fair." Explain when and with whom it is best to just keep quiet. They can always talk to you about it later.

Teaching a child to use "I messages" doesn't mean he always gets his way, just that he gets to say how he feels. If you're in a good mood, you may calmly reflect, "I know you don't think I'm fair, and I understand that you're mad. But this is the rule and you're stuck with it." The child knows you heard him; you acknowledged his feelings. And if he can say things like that to you, he has a better chance of stating his feelings and choices to a friend.

ASSERTIVENESS SKILLS

1. Make eye contact.

2. Use a firm, strong voice.

3. Say "NO" right away.

4. Say "NO" and walk away.

5. Say "NO" and invite the person to do something else.

6. Don't get into a discussion or an argument — you can't lose an argument you aren't in!

7. Don't defend yourself or make excuses.

8. Don't apologize. You aren't the one who is out of line!

9. Sound like your mind is made up!

10. Avoid situations where you are likely to be pressured.

11. Choose friends who respect your feelings.

12. Be a broken record. Just keep saying, "I understand what you want, but I'm not going to do it."

50 WAYS TO SAY NO TO DRUGS

1. "No, thanks."
2. "No way—my family would kill me!"
3. "No way—the teachers would kill me!"
4. "I gave it up for Lent."
5. "No thanks, I just had a bar of soap."
6. "I promised my family I wouldn't do that, and I keep my word."
7. "I don't want to. But thanks anyway."
8. "I don't want to. End of discussion."
9. "No way, Jose."
10. "I don't want to, and I can't believe that you want to get into that kind of stuff."
11. "My mind is made up. I don't want to talk about it any more."
12. "I'm not interested."
13. "If I did everything you wanted, I'd just be your puppet."
14. "I make my own decisions."
15. "If I have to do cigarettes, alcohol, or drugs to be your friend, then I guess I'll have to get a new friend."
16. "I'll pass."
17. "I like me the way I am."
18. "I don't need any."
19. "I'd rather save my brain for my other things."
20. "I'm not interested in getting high."
21. "I get my highs on mountains (or sports, or whatever)."
22. "I'm allergic to that stuff."
23. "Who needs it."
24. "It's not for me."
25. "I've got all the great feelings I need."
26. "I'm not into that."
27. "No, let's do something else."
28. "No, I've got things to do."
29. "I have plans later, and I need my brain."
30. "I'm trying to solve problems, not make more."
31. "I'll wait 'til it's proven safe."
32. "I have a different opinion."
33. "I don't like the lifestyle of people on drugs."
34. "No, my grades are bad enough."

35. "I don't want to take those kind of chances."
36. "I'm doing vitamins instead."
37. "You mean I have to smoke cigarettes (drink, or do drugs) to be your friend?"
38. "My body and I have a deal."
39. "I don't need that stuff to have fun."
40. "I can be spacey enough as it is."
41. "My memory has enough problems without that stuff."
42. "I said I wasn't interested. Now leave me alone."
43. "I don't have any brain cells to waste. I need them all."
44. "I have enough other ways to get into trouble."
45. "Are you crazy?"
46. "I have plans to stay healthy."
47. "I have other plans."
48. "I'd rather die of old age."
49. "No, I've heard about what that stuff can do to your brain."
50. "I'm happy without it."

ACTIVITIES FOR 50 WAYS TO SAY NO

1. Write "SAY NO TO DRUGS" vertically. Have the kids write a word or phrase for each line, starting with the letter on that line.
2. Make up a secret code. Write a message to remember if someone asks them to try tobacco, alcohol, or drugs. Kids can also illustrate the page. See if everyone can solve all the codes.

ASSERTIVENESS ACTIVITIES

1. Have the family make a list of things their friends pressure them to do. Then choose two volunteers to act out something from the list. One puts on the pressure, and the other is assertive. After you have acted out the scenario, discuss what might have been done differently. Then re-act the same scenario, only have the actors switch their roles. Again, discuss the role playing, and choose others to try the parts. Also, have them role play resisting cigarettes, alcohol, or drugs.
2. Have kids make posters, illustrating a rule for being assertive, or one of the ways to say "no."
3. Make a cartoon that shows kids saying "no."

4. Write a song or poem about kids saying no to cigarettes, alcohol, or drugs.
5. Write and put on a play about how to say no to cigarettes, alcohol, or drugs.
6. Make a comic strip showing people saying "no" to drugs.
7. Pantomime saying no to someone who is pantomiming trying to get you to do drugs.
8. Have kids make up a secret code and write a message to remember if someone asks them to try tobacco, alcohol, or drugs. Kids can also illustrate the page.

RECOMMENDED READING

(Some of these books are old, but the principles are tested and true. And children don't change every year like new cars!)

The Challenge of Child Training: A Parents' Guide; Rudolph Dreikurs; Hawthorne Books, Inc.; New York; 1972 Children: The Challenge; Rudolph Dreikurs; Hawthorne Books, Inc.; New York; 1964

Discipline Without Shouting or Spanking; Jerry Wyckoff & Barbara Unell; Meadowbrook Books; New York; 1984

For Love of the Children; Edward Ford & Steven Englund; Anchor Books; Garden City, NY; 1978

How to Say No and Keep Your Friends: Peer Pressure Reversal; Sharon Scott; Human Resource Development Press; Amherst, Massachusetts; 1987

Kids Can Cooperate, a Practical Guide to Teaching Problem Solving; Elizabeth Crary; Parenting Press; Seattle, Washington; 1984

A New Approach to Discipline: Logical Consequences; Rudolph Dreikurs & Loren Grey; Hawthorne Books, Inc.; New York; 1968

No-Fault Parenting; Helen Neville & Mona Halaby; The Body Press; Tuscon, AZ; 1984

Parent Effectiveness Training (also *Teacher Effectiveness Training*) Thomas Gordon; New American Library; New York; 1975

Parents in a Pressure Cooker; Jane Bluestein & Lynn Collins; I.S.S. Publications; Albuquerque, NM; 1983

Raising Kids O.K.; Dorothy E. Babcock & Terry D. Keepers; Avon Books; New York; 1976

When Your Child Drives You Crazy; Eda LeShan; St. Martin's Press; New York; 1985

Without Spanking or Spoiling, a Practical Approach to Toddler and Preschool Guidance; Elizabeth Crary; Parenting Press; Seattle, Washington; 1979

Yes, I Can Say No: A Parent's Guide to Assertiveness Training for Children; Manuel J. Smith; Arbor House; New York; 1986

Your Six Year Old (also books titled for ages 1,2,3,4, & 5); Louise Bates Ames & Frances L. Ilg; Dell Publishing; New York; 1976

Friends

It's a whole lot easier for children to say no to drugs if they have friends who are also saying no to drugs.

If children have self-esteem, confidence, and good friends, the battle is nearly won before it begins. Having the right friends builds confidence and self-worth, and vice-versa.

But do we teach children (or adults?!) how to make friends? Children will seek peer approval, and if they can't get it from the well-adjusted kids, they will get it from the losers. If they can't be "good enough" for the best, it's easy to be "bad enough" for the rest.

ACTIVITIES TO HELP CHILDREN MAKE FRIENDS

1. Discuss friendship. First, ask the kids what doesn't work. They will probably think of most of the following, and a few of their own ideas. Discuss why each idea doesn't work in the long run.
   A. Giving other kids money, candy, toys, etc.
   B. Bugging people to get their attention
   C. Hitting or kicking
   D. Stealing
   E. Tattling
   F. Name-calling

66

G. Interrupting

H. Being bossy

I. Put downs

J. Breaking people's things

K. Messing up others' work

L. Telling tales about other kids

M. Repeating things—"Do you know what Linda said about you?"

N. Preaching about "what you should do is..."

O. Bragging

P. Making up stories

Q. Bribing

R. Threatening

S. Making fun of them, their beliefs, or family rules

T. Trying to talk them into something they don't want to do or aren't allowed to do

Now, what does work?

A. Smile

B. Say "hi"

C. Invite someone to do something with you

D. Compliment

E. Ask opinions

F. Use their names

G. Share things

H. Share what you think and feel

I. Offer to help

J. Be considerate of their feelings

K. Accept their beliefs and family rules

L. Call them on the phone

2. Discuss: If someone says, "I won't be your friend unless you...," are they really your friend anyhow? Do you want to be a puppet with someone else deciding what you do?

3. Act out how to make friends, how not to make friends, and how to deal with problems from friends. Children can role play both parts, and then discuss how the interaction went. Each of

the above points can be acted out, a few each day. Or set aside one day a week to spends ten minutes on the subject.

4. Have something like a "Dear Ann Landers" box, where children deposit letters about their concerns in making good friends. These can be used for discussions.

5. Put on a play about making friends. Use puppets or dolls or stuffed animals. Use two children, or one child can play both parts—they do this all the time when they play, anyhow.

6. Ask the kids what you can say to compliment someone besides, "You're nice," "You're fun," "You're cute," and all the other over-used phrases. Write down their ideas. Then give every child a piece of paper to fold into twelfths. Kids ask each other and you to write on it, similar to an autograph book, except the kids write a compliment.

   Challenge them to write something personal and different for everyone. It might be something like, "I liked the joke you told at recess," or "You have a nice soft voice." Try to write something yourself for every kid. If you're a teacher, you'll suddenly realize who you don't know very well, when you look at a child's paper and can't think of anything personal that you can sincerely say. It happens to the best of us.

7. Let the kids make posters about how to make friends.

8. Everyone pick a family member and make a poster about another family member that shows what's good about him.

9. Make up stories about a friendless kid who learns how to make friends.

10. Play a game, using the kids' initials. They have to think of an adjective that starts with the first letter of their name. The first person introduces himself. The next person identifies the first and then adds their own introduction, and so on.

    Example: "I'm smiling Susan." "That's smiling Susan and I'm artistic Al."

11. Have a discussion topic, "I'm friends with _____ because
    _____." At the end, summarize the qualities discussed, and
    how to be a good friend.

12. Write a book, How to Make Friends. (Use the list at the begin-
    ning of this section, or the kids can write their own.) Kids can
    add a page a day. Each child can make his own book, or each
    child can make a page in a book for the family.

13. Make a greeting card for someone and tell him something you
    like about him. Be sure everyone gets a card or two.

RECOMMENDED READING

Helping Kids Make Friends; Holly S. Stocking, Diana Arezzo, &
Shelly Leavitt; Boys Town Center for the Study of Youth Development

*Relationship Builders: 156 Activities and Games for Building Rela-
tionships;* Joy Wilt & Bill Watson; Word, Inc.; Waco, Texas; 1978

Communication and Drug Prevention

Studies indicate that children are less apt to use drugs if the family is warm, affectionate, and communicative. By developing communication at home, children are given a better chance to develop the skills to "say no."

It is critical that this whole process be accepting and non-judgmental! If a child tells you he's curious and wants to try drugs, do you suppose he'll change his mind just because he gets a serious lecture and/or a disapproving expression? More likely, he will clam up and you will never again experience that degree of honesty.

The principle holds true for less extreme examples. If you want kids to talk to you, they have to know that it's safe to do so. Advising, putting down, dominating, intimidating, judging, and interrupting all interfere with the long term goal, and if done regularly, will actually increase the likelihood of later substance abuse!!

That doesn't mean you approve of whatever is said. You can tell them, "I hope you don't because drugs hurt you, but I appreciate your honesty in telling me."

Usually, the most effective response is to parrot back what you heard, and maybe tag on a feeling you imagine the child has. If a child says, "The only way I'd do drugs is if all my friends did," an appropriate response is, "You don't want to feel left out. You might do drugs so you wouldn't feel left out?" Children must first

70

feel they are understood and accepted as they are now, before they have freedom to really change. If they spend energy trying to defend or deny who they are now, internal change is almost impossible.

At the end of each discussion, it is valuable to ask children what they learned. Often a child discovers that a lot of people feel just like he does — and what a relief that is!

ACTIVITIES TO IMPROVE COMMUNICATIONS

On the following pages are discussion topics for the family. The kids can make a writing book. Each day after the discussions, the kids can write their own answers to the topic.

The questions here are just a sample of what'spossible. Children love to make up their own. These are just a starting point.

1. I made a good choice when I . . .
2. I made a bad choice when I . . .
3. I knew I'd get in trouble, but I did it anyway because. . .
4. I knew I'd get in trouble, so I didn't do it because. . .
5. Why do people drink, smoke, and do drugs?
6. My friends talked me into it.
7. My friends tried to talk me into it, but I said no.
8. I would never . . . because. . .
9. I need help with. . .
10. I feel good when. . .
11. If my best friend started to take drugs, I would. . .
12. What would you do if someone offered you drugs?
13. I took the risk because. . .
14. I didn't take the risk because. . .
15. What are the risks and possible consequences of smoking, drinking, and drugs?
16. How do you decide if something is good or bad for you?
17. What do people tell you is good about cigarettes, alcohol, and drugs?
18. Does everyone older than you know more than you? How do you decide if they're right?
19. Should you always do what older kids and adults tell you? When should you "do what you're told"?
20. What do people say to make you feel bad if you say "no" to what they want you to do?

21. I was talked into it.
22. I did it so he/she would like me.
23. I did it to impress someone.
24. I did it because I didn't want to feel left out.
25. I feel bad when...
26. When I feel bad, I want to...
27. I can make myself feel better if I...
28. I feel guilty when...
29. When I'm tired of feeling guilty, I...
30. I would be happier if...
31. If I want to get my way with my parents, I...
32. When my parents are mad...
33. I can get out of trouble by...
34. I used to pretend it wasn't a problem.
35. I feel strong when...
36. I feel independent when...
37. I feel trusted when...
38. I feel attractive when...
39. I feel grown-up when...
40. I feel important when...
41. I wish my parents would...
42. I wish my teachers would...
43. I wish my parents wouldn't...
44. I wish my teachers wouldn't...
45. I can really talk to...because...
46. I can't talk to...because...
47. I know I'm important to...because...
48. The most important people to me are...
49. People who drink and/or do drugs act...
50. People who drink and/or do drugs feel...
51. We wouldn't have drug or alcohol problems if...
52. I hate to...
53. I could do better if...
54. My parents say...
55. My teacher says...
56. People like me because...
57. I hope I can...
58. Someone did something that made me feel good.59. I was happy when...

60. It's fun to imagine...
61. It was so funny when...
62. I was proud of myself when...
63. I didn't feel the way I expected to when...
64. In my free time I like to...
65. If I could do whatever I wanted...
66. I thought of the answer to the problem!
67. I can't wait!
68. I tried hard, but it didn't turn out the way I planned
69. I felt different after I thought about it.
70. I planned it and it was great!

RECOMMENDED READING

Between Parent and Child; Haim Ginott; Macmillan Company; New York; 1965

How to Talk So Kids Will Listen & Listen So Kids Will Talk; Adele Faber & Elaine Mazlish; Avon Books; New York, New York; 1980

Parent Effectiveness Training (or *Teacher Effectiveness Training*) Thomas Gordon; New American Library; NY; 1975

TV's False Promises and the Drug Problem

This is not going to be a popular idea, but a great deal of the drug problem is related to our TV addiction. And if you don't believe you're addicted, try giving it up for a month! Those who have done so, as participants in research experiments, claim many positive changes in their life and quality of family interactions — and as soon as the month is up, they eagerly return to their previous TV addiction, in spite of their new awareness!

The Weekly Reader Survey found that TV and movies have the greatest influence in making substance abuse attractive to fourth graders. Older children ranked this influence second only to other children.

Commercials tell us we should not be uncomfortable for any longer than it takes to swallow some pills. They also learn that serious problems can be easily solved in 30-60 minutes. Relationships become wonderfully satisfying during a twenty to forty minute program. Thoroughly disgusting characters see the evil of their ways and turn over a new leaf — or they get killed and are no longer an issue. You don't see problems and neurotic people who tenaciously continue to plague, annoy, and stress the main character. By the end of the program, everything is usually wonderful. And even if it's a tragedy, the resolution is very clear. You don't see people spending years in therapy resolving personal problems and developing life skills. You miss the reality that it takes years in college or other training to develop career skills. TV paints a false picture of instant success in careers and relationships. Has real life been like that for you?

In addition, TV is a quick, easy way to feel good. Kids learn they can feel good without any effort to solve their problems. Just turn on the tube and tune out real life. Get wrapped up in the show and your own bleak existence vanishes. If you don't think kids get wrapped up in TV, just try to get their attention while their eyes are glued to an exciting part of the show. Do they ever get so wrapped up in reading, conversation, or doing their homework that they become oblivious to someone walking into the room or speaking to them?

And worst of all, the time kids spend watching TV is time not spent developing life skills, like coping and socializing. Kids who grow up with an electronic baby sitter don't get as much experience interacting with others.

Some kids say they just want the TV on all the time for the background noise. But the brain is only capable of higher level thinking, such as meaning, purpose, hindsight, perception, judgment planning, commitment and empathy during quiet times. Is constant background noise healthy? And what is it about silence that is so uncomfortable? Could it be they are afraid their own thoughts and feelings might plow into their conscious minds? Isn't that the same reason people become alcoholics or use drugs regularly? We must solve problematic causes, not just chase elusive symptoms.

ACTIVITIES TO TEACH TV-COPING SKILLS

1. Have the kids watch a fictional TV show or a movie. Discuss all the things that were unrealistic. They may find too many coincidences, too many easy solutions, or miraculous changes in people. Then tell the kids to write the story as it would probably happen in real life. (Remember, true stories aren't worthy of broadcast unless they are very unusual compared to how things normally happen in real life!)

2. Tell the kids to keep a log of their TV watching. Write down what they watched, why they watched it, the time of day, how they felt when they turned the TV on and off, and what they would have done instead if the TV were broken. Have them do this for seven days.

3. Ask everyone to give up TV for a week, or if they dare, for a month. First, have them make a list of shows or times they normally watch TV. Mark the times that it will be the hardest for them to do something else. Then make a list of other things they can do instead of watching TV. Tell them to save their favorite things for those times. Keep a log of what they do instead, and how they feel. If they cheat and do watch a program, they should write down why they decided to watch it anyway, how they felt when they made the decision, and how they felt later. And remember, all the reasons for watching TV (with the possible exception of educational programming) are the same reasons people use tobacco, alcohol, and drugs.

4. Discuss why TV and movies are so unrealistic. Why are there so few true stories being filmed?

5. Have kids write or draw pictures of what they can do instead of watching TV.

6. Discuss what you see people doing on a TV show. Talk about the things that are good, and the things that are bad.

7. Discuss all of the commercials everyone can think of. Talk about which ones succeed in making you want the advertised product.

8. Have kids list all the drugs they see in TV programs and commercials. Have them categorize them into: (1) prescription, (2) over the counter, (3) illegal drugs, and (4) socially acceptable but not healthy (caffeine, alcohol, and nicotine are drugs!)

RECOMMENDED READING

The Plug-In Drug; Marie Winn; 1985; Viking

The Plug-In Drug: Television, Children, and the Family; Marie Winn; 1985; Penguin

Unplugging the Plug-In Drug; Marie Winn; 1987; Penguin

Unplugging the Plug-In Drug: Help Your children Kick the TV Habit; Marie Winn; 1987; Viking

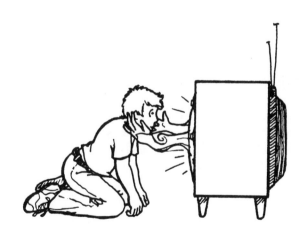

Nutrition: A Well-Kept Secret to Drug-Proofing

Believe it or not, many experts believe nutrition plays a vital part in preventing drug abuse. According to Dr. Donald Land, a nutritional consultant specializing in addiction, you will have emotional and psychological problems caused by nutritional deficiencies long before you have any physical symptoms. And you can have these problems without ever developing the physical symptoms caused by a more severe deficiency. So if all you care about is getting the minimum daily requirements, i.e., minimum health, you ensure that you will have emotional and psychological problems that people accept as "normal." If you want Grade A physical and mental health, then excellent nutrition and vitamin and mineral supplements are important considerations.

Kids with poor nutrition and lots of junk food are much more likely to do drugs. Not all of them will, of course. But kids who start drugs are seldom the ones with good nutrition. Developing healthy eating habits is just one more thing you can do to increase the odds in your child's favor.

With the current trend to have candy and soda pop machines in every school, it makes you aware of how important money is. The schools could sell healthy snacks, if they cared about nutrition and good eating habits more than money.

Any health book will provide ample information for basic nutrition, so that will not be covered in this book, beyond a reminder: 3 servings from the milk and dairy group, 2 servings from the meat and eggs group, 4 servings from the fruit and vegetables group, and 4 servings from the bread and cereal group.

For advice on vitamins, minerals, herbs, etc., see your local health food store. Many have excellent books on the subject, if you want to learn more.

Your doctor and the American Medical Association are not likely to agree with anything in this section of the book, especially the following. After all, they only make money if you have problems. But if your child is hyperactive or has behavior problems, and your doctor's only recommendation is drugs or "tough it out," there are some alternatives.

A rare but important consideration is allergies that cause emotional/behavioral problems. Although some say they are not allergies in the strictest definition, these sensitivities have terrible effects on some children (and their families who must live with them!). The discomforts and problems caused by these allergies will put these children at risk for later drug abuse.

Intolerance to foods can cause severe behavior problems. Common culprits are: milk (25% of white children, especially blue-eyed blonds, and 75% of non-white children cannot tolerate milk), wheat, gluten, chocolate, eggs, corn, peanuts, meat, orange juice, and sugar. Problems may include extreme fussiness, prolonged crying, or outright screaming in younger children, and out-of-control, sometimes even violent behavior, in older ones.

Preservatives, artificial flavors and colors, as well as natural salicylates (which occur in tomatoes, cucumbers, almonds, apples, apricots, berries, cherries, currants, grapes, nectarines, oranges, peaches, plums, and prunes) cause hyperactivity in many children, especially boys.

While research is still young, early experiments in diet with behaviorally disturbed children have been quite successful. Often as many as 75% of the children improve with the elimination of allergens from their diet. Many have suddenly improved in school work and learning ability as well. And children who do well in school are less likely to turn to drugs.

If you think you're really open-minded, read on about this rare occurrence. Chris was a toddler with all of the above allergies — the kind of kid you might be tempted to throw out the window after listening to him scream for six hours. When the previously mentioned allergens were removed from his diet, he became normal, even sunny, in his disposition. However, he remained delayed in his mental development, could not understand even the simplest language, and had absolutely no problem-solving skills.

The parent was told of a chiropractor who had supposedly relieved allergy problems in young children. Skeptical but desperate, figuring there was nothing to lose and it couldn't hurt to have the kid's spine correctly aligned, the mother brought the little boy in to give it a try. After two weeks, the child gradually began eating regular food, and two months later, had absolutely no dietary restrictions.

The doctor also recommended taking the child to another chiropractor who was certified in craniology. After a few adjustments, the tot began to talk, understood and followed simple directions, and grew mentally by leaps and bounds.

Two other documented physical problems were also corrected by the treatment from these same doctors.

Pretty incredible. Hard to believe. Call it coincidence, but it's hard not to respect doctors who can predict coincidence. The only thing that matters is the little boy is still doing great over a year later. He is now quite normal.

ACTIVITIES TO TEACH GOOD NUTRITION

1. Have children cut out pictures of food from newspapers or magazines, to be pasted onto a poster illustrating the four food groups or five...if you want to include "junk food," often more politely called "other." This may help children become aware of how much non-nutritious food is available, especially if they are cutting out pictures from magazines.

2. Have children keep a log of everything they eat or drink for one week. At the end of each day's listing, they should label how much food they had from each group, and whether they needed any different foods to have a balanced diet. The purpose is awareness.

3. Children can plan a week's menus of healthy foods they like.

4. Children can make place mats showing the four food groups. Cover them with clear contact paper, so the spills can be wiped up. Just don't put them in the dishwasher!

5. Children can decorate a box (to be used for storage or as their own personal trash can) that shows the four food groups — one group on each side of the box.

6. Tell the kids to pick a food and think of all the ways it can be cooked.

7. Have the kids collect pictures of meals. Then, decide how many servings there are from each food group, and if any food group was omitted.

8. Have the kids cut out pictures of food. On the back of each picture, write which food group(s) it belongs to. Then make a bag for each food group, and bags for combinations of 2, 3, or all 4 food groups. Let the kids sort the food into the right bag. Since the answers are on the back, this will be a self-checking activity, and no one will practice the wrong answers.

RECOMMENDED READING

Allergies and the Hyperactive Child; Doris J. Rapp; Simon & Schuster, Cornerstone Library; New York; 1979

Brain Allergies; William H. Philpott & Dwight K. Kalita; Keats Publishing, Inc.; New Canaan, Connecticut; 1980

Dr. Mandell's 5-Day Allergy Relief System; Dr. Marshall Mandell & Lynne Waller Scanion; Pocket Books; New York; 1979

Earl Mindell's Vitamin Bible; Earl Mindell; Warner Books; New York; 1979

Earl Mindell's Vitamin Bible for Kids; Earl Mindell; Bantam Books; New York; 1981

Feed Your Kids Right; Lendon Smith; Delta Publishing Company; New York; 1979

Fighting for Tony; Mary Callahan; Simon & Schuster; 1987

Food, Mind, & Mood; David Sheinkin, Michael Schachter, & Richard Hutton; Warner Books; 1979

How to Control Your Allergies; Robert Forman; Larchmont Books; New York; 1979

Improve Your Child's Behavior Chemistry; Lendon H. Smith; Prentice-Hall, Inc.; Englewood Cliffs, NJ; 1984

When Children Invite Child Abuse; Svea J. Gold; Fern Ridge Press; Eugene, Oregon; 1986

Why Your Child Is Hyperactive; Ben F. Feingold; Random House; New York; 1975

How to be Happy
Without Drugs

It seldom occurs to anyone that being happy is something you can *learn*. We tend to think of happiness as a mystical quality that comes to some, and not others, based on external situations. The poor think they need to be rich. The rich think they need love. The loved think they need to have more status. Others think their lives are no fun, or they aren't healthy enough. Whatever most people have, they feel they're missing something vital. While some of life is affected by externals that we can't control, most of the things that directly affect us are within our control or influence.

Most of our "poor me-ness" is caused by the focus we put on what we can't have or do. Ironically, it seems the more kids have — especially without working for it — the more they want and the less happy they are! The lack of a normal frustration tolerance is a big problem. Kids have never had so much, nor felt so lacking. The numbers are worn right off their parents' credit cards in search of children's happiness. Kids can't tolerate the frustration of waiting or doing without. They have to have it, and they have to have it now. Instead of moaning over what life is lacking, kids can learn to brainstorm for the positives *they* can add to their lives, and maybe learn to appreciate better what they already have.

To be happy, children need to be loved, trusted, have fun,

acceptance, confidence, and to generally feel good about themselves and life. They also need to know how to deal with negative feelings. Getting all the things they want is optional, and possibly a distraction from learning how to make themselves happy.

If children are happy, they are more apt to "just say no" to drugs. Drug users do not have a reputation for overflowing with the joy of life. They typically turn to drugs or alcohol as a feeble attempt to meet one of their basic needs — one they weren't meeting in a healthy way. Children who feel left out and friendless will do anything to change this, and if drugs will get them accepted into a group of people, by golly, they're very likely to give it a try. That is one of the most common reasons drug users give for starting drugs.

Children need to learn that if they can't have exactly what they want, there are other options besides being miserable and unhappy. Maybe their parents won't let them have a dog or cat, but there might be other pets they *can* have. Maybe they can have a gerbil, or a fish. Or maybe they can find someone who needs to have his dog walked, and they can be friends and play with that dog. That's not their first choice by a long shot, but something that will help meet the need. It's a whole lot better than being miserable.

ACTIVITIES TO TEACH
HAPPINESS WITHOUT DRUGS

1. Kids can make a diorama of what they can do so they won't need tobacco, alcohol, or drugs.

2. Have the kids make a mobile of things they enjoy doing, so they can be happy and not need tobacco, alcohol, or drugs.

3. Kids can make a poster of how they can have fun outside the tobacco, alcohol, or drug scene.

4. Kids need to know how to deal honestly with negative feelings to be really happy. Tell the kids to think of a time they were really angry. Then have them write or draw a picture of what they felt like doing when they were so angry. When each child is done, he can wad up the paper, jump on it, tear it into shreds, and then throw it away, along with his angry feelings.

(Unless the kids are talking seriously about their feelings, there should be no conversation. If they are laughing and joking, they aren't dealing with their anger. Laughing, when used to avoid feelings, interferes with learning to be happy.)

5. Have the kids spend a few minutes each day writing in their feelings book. Give them a copy of the feeling words on page 32. Encourage them to use these words in describing how they feel and what they learned each day. Once a month, have the children read everything they have written. Tell them to write how they feel about things now that some time has passed.

HOW I CAN BE HAPPY WITHOUT CIGARETTES, ALCOHOL, OR DRUGS

Children write or draw pictures for each page. Young children will probably only have a few answers for each page, while older children can be encouraged to brainstorm as many valid answers as possible. Discuss each topic and possible answers before asking the children to do their own page. One page a day is preferable. Many children will like this so much they will want to do it all at once, but it is better to give them practice every day in learning to think this way. If they do it all at once, answers tend to be quick and shallow. Daily practice increases the likelihood that this skill will be internalized.

1. If someone doesn't love me, I know these people DO love me.
2. If someone doesn't like me, I know these people DO like me a lot.
3. If I need help, these people would help me even if they don't know me.
4. I'm not good at everything, but I am good at these things.
5. I like me best when...
6. I can't do it now, but when I am older, I want to...
7. Sometimes I have to work, but when I have free time, I like to...
8. People, groups, organizations I belong with...
9. My favorite things to do...

10. I have things I like very much.
11. I know some important facts.
12. I believe some important ideas.
13. Things I can do to be healthy...
14. Sometimes I'm not happy. I can cheer myself up by...
15. People I spend a lot of time with...
16. Sometimes, when my friends are all busy, I could call someone new, like...
17. Ways I can make new friends...
18. Sometimes there's no one to do anything with. Things I can enjoy when I'm alone are...
19. If things are going wrong, I can count on my family to...
20. When I don't have much money, I can...
21. Mistakes I'm not going to make...
22. When I don't know something, I can find out by...
23. The most important things in life are...
24. The best things about me are...
25. People I can trust if I need help are...

RECOMMENDED READING

Happiness: It's Your Choice; Gary Applegate; Berringer Publishing; Sherman Oaks, CA; 1985

Risk Taking —
What Are the Odds and
Is It Worth the Risk?

Willingness to risk is a very personal matter, and varies with each person according to the nature of the risk. Some kids are true daredevils with physical risks, but much too shy to risk participating in a class discussion, which is an emotional risk.

The critical factors to consider in making decisions are: (1) What are the possible risks?, (2) What is the probability of undesirable results, and (3) What is the value to be gained by taking the risk?

In deciding to tell a joke, you risk possible embarrassment if no one laughs. In taking drugs, you risk instant death — or a slow, painful death through irreversible deterioration. We risk death every time we get in a car, but the probability is low enough that the advantages far outweigh the risk.

Children need to be aware of their strengths and weaknesses in risk taking. If a child realizes that he is exceedingly cautious in social risks, but failure in this area is not usually fatal, it may help him gather the courage to try saying "hello" to someone he hasn't met yet. If a child understands that he is very comfortable with physical risks, he might learn to stop and think before deciding to accept the dare to cross the raging river by walking across a pipeline. Physical challenges may not be frightening, even if the risk of harm is quite high. Kids need to learn when to restrain themselves, and when to push themselves. The goal is not to avoid all risks, just the ones where the potential harm outweighs the potential good.

If you try something new, such as calling someone on the phone or participating more in class, the worst thing that is likely to happen is that someone might think or say something you won't like. The possible good outweighs the possible harm. It's a reasonable risk to take.

However, if you want to try riding a horse, and the only horse available is a very young, untrained, spirited horse, and you have never ridden before, then the odds are quite high that you will fall off. You probably won't like it and you might get hurt. It would not be smart to try it. It is important to think things through before making a decision.

RISK-TAKING ACTIVITIES

1. Discuss risks family members have taken, how things turned out, and how they feel about their choices.

2. Watch a TV show, movie, or read a book and list the physical, social, and emotional risks that the characters took, and the outcomes. Discuss which risks were reasonable and which were stupid. Did the characters have other choices that might have been better? Which of these risks would the kids be willing to take if they were in the same situation?

3. Have the kids make a list of risks in their life. Write down the worst things that are likely to happen. For example, if they wear a new shirt and no one likes it, the worst thing that is likely to happen is they might be embarrassed and never wear it again. The other "worst thing" is they wasted their money when they bought it. It is very unlikely that they will actually die from this risk.

On the other hand, if they decided to rob a bank, the worst thing that would probably happen is they would get caught and go to juvenile jail. They would lose most of their freedom and might have a miserable life. It is also possible that they could get killed by someone who doesn't like bank robbers.

4. Have the kids make puppets and put on a puppet show about a risk that one of them is considering.

TYPES OF RISKS

Discuss whether each of the items on the following list seems like a big risk, no risk, or somewhere in between. The answer may be different for each family member. What scares us is highly individual.

At the end of the exercise, it is good to discuss what the children learned. Have the children decide whether they are stronger in taking emotional or physical risks. Have them pick an item from each category and discuss why it is easy or hard for them.

After the exercise, everyone should pick something from this page (or make up their own) that is a reasonable risk that they would be willing to try. Write down what you will do and when, and how you think it will feel. Rehearse it mentally, thinking about how well it will turn out. It should be a risk that is not likely to send anyone to the hospital! If it involves saying something to another person, and it's really hard for them (such as saying how they feel about him), and it's just too hard to do, they might send a note or card with a written compliment.

After everyone has taken their risk, discuss what everyone did, if it turned out differently than planned, how the person reacted (if another person was involved), how they felt doing it, and how they feel now that it's done.

Do this every day for a week. And don't forget to breathe!

RISKS:

__ answering the phone at home
__ answering the phone at school
__ going off the high diving board
__ jumping into the shallow end of the pool
__ saying hello to a child you don't know

89

___ saying hello to an adult you don't know
___ taking an adult on a tour of your school
___ rock climbing
___ selling candy to your friends and family
___ selling candy door-to-door
___ answering a question in class
___ standing up in front of the class and talking
___ climbing up a steep cliff
___ being in a school play
___ singing with a group of children
___ singing alone in front of an audience
___ riding a horse while standing in the saddle
___ going to a scary movie that might give you nightmares
___ introducing yourself to the new kid on the block
___ parachuting
___ getting a new hair style
___ wearing the latest style in clothing
___ wearing what you like, even if it's not in style
___ going to the doctor
___ going to the dentist
___ hang gliding
___ talking to the counselor about a personal problem
___ talking to your teacher
___ talking to your parents
___ trying to jump across a babbling brook
___ floating down a fast moving river on a raft
___ swimming in a pool
___ swimming under water
___ swimming in the ocean
___ riding in a row boat
___ riding in a canoe
___ riding in a motor boat
___ holding a snake
___ picking up a spider
___ putting a worm on a fishhook
___ going to a school dance
___ taking care of the neighbor's new baby
___ learning to dance
___ learning karate

___ sending a Valentine to a boyfriend or a girlfriend
___ saying "I love you" to your family
___ saying "I love you" to someone not in your family
___ reading a book of your choice
___ saying "no" to your friends
___ reading aloud in the classroom
___ taking a message to the principal
___ having an operation
___ going to a party with a lot of friends
___ going to a party where you don't know anyone
___ apologizing
___ confessing something you did, when no one would know
___ telling the truth when you might get away with a lie
___ telling a bully to leave the little kid alone
___ telling an adult you disagree with what they did
___ asking your parents for money
___ saying "no" to your friends
___ talking about what you think
___ talking about how you feel
___ telling someone why you like them
___ making a suggestion to the principal
___ having your picture taken
___ talking into a tape recorder
___ talking into a microphone
___ skiing
___ playing softball
___ roller skating
___ giving a flower to a friend
___ lending money to a friend
___ lending one of your favorite things to a friend
___ entering a contest
___ trying a cigarette
___ having a beer
___ trying drugs
___ writing about yourself
___ talking about yourself
___ drawing
___ having your work on the school bulletin board
___ showing your report card to your family

RECOMMENDED READING

Risking; David Viscott; Pocket Books; New York; 1977

Decision Making —
Making Good Decisions
Means Saying No to Drugs

Children with adequate decision making skills are better able to decide to say "no" to drugs. Decision making is an important skill that is used throughout our lives. We make hundreds of decisions every day — whether to call in sick, to try to make that yellow light, to grab a quick snack, how to deal with problems at home and on the job...the list goes on endlessly. But how often is time spent teaching this essential skill of decision making?

Making children aware of good and bad choices in a friendly, non-threatening discussion helps them build decision making skills. Children can learn a lot just by the way we deal with everyday problems. If a child has been in a fight, a lecture is not necessary. Instead, ask the child what new problems were caused by that choice, and what he could do differently next time that might turn out better. The fact that this is a "friendly discussion" does not eliminate consequences — in fact, it shows children the consequences they've brought on themselves. Discipline is essential and can motivate younger children to make good choices!

Structured decision making is helpful for decisions that can be thought out in advance. A child may be trying to decide whether to

93

buy a banana split today, or save the money towards a toy or a tape player he wants. The child can write down the reasons he wants each item, and the disadvantages of each choice. Then he can mark the reasons that are most important to him, possibly by giving points to each reason, including negative points for the disadvantages.

Often the longest list of reasons to buy a given thing is not "the winner"—the reasons on the long list could all be of minor importance. The other choice could have only a few, but very significant, reasons. Or one may have a single disadvantage that totally outweighs all other factors (like if you take drugs, you will damage your brain).

Taking the example of banana split versus a toy or tape player, the following thoughts might occur to the child:

Banana Split

GOOD
It tastes yummy.
All my friends are going for ice cream.
I have enough money today.
I'm bored and want something to do.

DISADVANTAGES
It only lasts about 20 minutes.
It'll be even longer before I can get the toy or tape player.

Toy or Tape Player

GOOD
It'll be fun.
It lasts a long time.
I can enjoy it with my friends.
I can enjoy it when I'm alone.

DISADVANTAGES
I have to wait and keep saving for several weeks.
If I save all my money for the toy or tape player, I won't be able to buy ice cream with my friends.

In this case, the chart came out with an even number of good and bad points, so weighing the items becomes even more important. Maybe having fun with friends is the most important thing. In that case, the child may decide to buy an ice cream cone instead of a banana split, and save the difference towards his long term goal. Regardless of his choice, the child is aware of his options and his feelings, and makes his choice based on reason.

In the above choice, the child has all the necessary information. In some choices, getting more information about his choices is the first step. Other times, brainstorming all his options may have to be done first.

Learning decision making skills also develops the concept of long and short term goals. People often define maturity as the ability to sacrifice short term for long term goals. But this is not a matter of age. There are three-year-olds who choose to only spend some of their allowance today, saving the rest for other days. If the child can talk, he's not too young to start learning this skill.

DECISION MAKING ACTIVITIES

1. Ask children to evaluate the advantages and disadvantages of a choice between a trip to Disneyland or having their very own TV and VCR in their room (or whatever choices would be meaningful to your children.) Have them list the factors to consider, and to weight them. Each child will have his own list. There are no absolute reasons or disadvantages. Different children will make different decisions. Stress that there are no right or wrong answers. The only thing is to think of how you feel and why, and not to overlook anything! Even reasons that seem silly are important and need to be included.

   Be accepting and non-judgmental about the children's feelings. If a child said a disadvantage of going to Disneyland would be having to bring his sister, that's how he feels. A lecture on brotherly love and sharing will only teach the child to be less honest in the future — which is the opposite of teaching how to make good decisions.

2. Ask the children if they would like a chocolate or a vanilla cookie. Write down their choices. The next day, fill their orders. But the chocolate cookies are tiny and not very good. The vanilla cookies are huge, with frosting and sprinkles. They are delicious. Ask the children what they learned about making decisions. Many answers are possible, but the obvious is: "Sometimes you need to get more information about your choices before making a decision." Assumptions can lead to disappointment.

3. Have children find ads on two similar items they wish they could buy, like two different bikes. Have them critique the ads, finding out how much information is supplied, what further information they would want to find out, and what factors would help them decide which bike to buy.

4. Pretend someone asks you to try drugs with them. Although in real life, you wouldn't say, "Wait, I have to make a chart of the advantages and disadvantages before I make my choice," do this now just for practice. Even if they know absolutely what their answer would be, it's good to think it through just to sharpen their thinking skills.

5. Brainstorming is often the way to make a decision easier. Kids may think of an option that's perfect, but it just didn't occur to them at first. Suppose they need money to go to a special show with their friends, and it's only going to be here for one week. How many ways can they think of to earn money?

RECOMMENDED READING

Teach Your Child Decision Making; John F. Clabby, Ph.D., and Maurice J. Elias, Ph.D.; Doubleday & Company, Inc.; New York, 1987.

Drug-Proofing Young Children

Young children need to know that the only good drugs are those their parents (or doctor or nurse) give them when they are sick. And unless there are unusual health problems, they should know that the medicine is only for a short time. It's not good to take medicine all the time. They need to learn while they're young and "righteous" (before age 8) that it's not good to smoke or drink. Alcohol and tobacco are the enticers that children start with, before pot and other drugs. Children who don't drink or smoke probably won't do drugs either.

The focus with young children must be on the short term effects. If fear of cancer or cirrhosis was an effective deterrent, the alcohol and tobacco industries would be out of business. The long term effects don't stop many adults, and it certainly won't stop kids. Like adults, they say, "It won't happen to me," or "I don't care what happens when I'm old, I want to have fun now." And most kids know people who do drugs and have never jumped out of a window or gone crazy or died.

Tell young children and pre-adolescents that if they smoke, they'll smell like an ashtray — and let them take a whiff. Tell them smoking will make them cough and feel sick. They might even throw up the first time. Tell them if they drink, they'll have trouble thinking. They might have an accident. They may do something stupid and embarrass everyone — and be embarrassed themselves when they find out what they did.

You can begin drug-proofing children when they are three or four. Before fourth grade, almost all children will say, "I'd never do that!" This self-talk will be a hundred times more effective than you telling them not to do it. Talk about it often, so they can practice thinking "I'd never do that." When they watch TV or movies, make negative comments about smoking and drinking, without preaching. Just comment, "How do you think that cigarette smells?" "How does he act when he's drunk? Do you think that's a very smart thing to do?"

As kids get older, it will be much harder, if not impossible, to influence their thinking. Remember, children who make and reaffirm their own decisions years before the peer pressure hits (usually in fourth grade), are most likely to say no to drugs.

Kids, even three-year-olds, want to feel strong, attractive, independent, liked, and even grown up. If you do everything you can to help them feel that way through healthy activities and honest, positive comments, then later they will not need tobacco, alcohol, or drugs to give the illusion of these qualities.

Children (and adults!) need to feel valued. If this sense of being valued does not come from home or school, guess where the kids will find it.

Parents need to stay involved with PTA/PTO, school conferences, and other community awareness programs. Showing an active, supporting (but not pushy or demanding) interest in education helps keep kids on the right track.

If you smoke, tell the kids it was a mistake to start: you wish you didn't, but you just can't quit. Tell them you know that most kids copy their parents, but you hope they don't make the same mistake of smoking.

If you're a light social drinker, discuss the difference between that and children who drink. Tell them you drink responsibly and legally — and you don't drive if you've had more than two. Children who drink illegally are more like adults who drink irresponsibly, and like alcoholics who drink to feel better. They want to run away from their problems, but they just make new ones. Happy children don't drink. Happy adults don't abuse alcohol.

The biggest reason kids shouldn't use tobacco, alcohol, or drugs is their brains are still growing. Children's and teenagers' brains are much more seriously damaged by even small amounts of experimenting. In adults, tobacco primarily hurts their respiratory system. For kids, there is brain damage as well. Any use of tobacco, alcohol, or drugs will cause some level of damage in kids, limiting their emotional development and thinking skills. Kids who use will never mature fully. The greater the use, the greater the damage.

Discuss that on TV and in movies, they will see people having fun smoking, drinking, and doing drugs. But this kind of fun is risky. Talk about the reasons people do these things, while they're young enough to believe they'd say no. They'll hear it later from kids, so it's best if they have heard and discussed it first with you. Don't send them to battle unarmed!

Starting around age three, listen to kids' feelings, thoughts, and concerns about cigarettes, drugs, and alcohol. Discuss and provide information, but don't argue or preach, or they won't talk to you.

Make sure kids understand that they can tell you if someone offers them cigarettes, alcohol, or drugs. They need to talk about what happened and have your support. Assure them they did the right thing by saying no and telling you.

ACTIVITIES FOR VERY YOUNG CHILDREN

1. Discuss with your child what he should taste. Take him through the house (in the garage and outside, too) and ask him, "Should you taste this?" Unless the child remembers you, or another responsible adult, giving it to him to eat, he should say no.

Also discuss how he should handle each of the following:

A. a friend gives him candy
B. a stranger gives him candy
C. he finds candy (how does he know it's candy and not pills?)
D. you or the babysitter give him medicine
E. his friends give him medicine
F. you find medicine

G. a doctor or nurse gives you medicine

H. you find something and don't know what it is

2. Give your kids magazines to cut out pictures of things that have a drug in them. Remember — alcohol, caffeine, and nicotine are drugs, too. Things to look for include:

   A. beer
   B. champagne
   C. cigar
   D. wine
   E. cigarettes
   F. coffee
   G. tobacco in a pipe
   H. tea
   I. chewing tobacco

3. Help your kids make a book called *I Won't Smoke Because*. Each child can make his own book, or can make a page to be duplicated and compiled into a family book.

4. Have your kids make a picture, "Save Our Lungs." Kids can illustrate and/or write reasons why they don't want to breathe smoke — their own or others.

5. Tell your kids to make a "stay well" card for themselves. Inside, they can write down the important things they want to remember.

RECOMMENDED READING:

It's O.K. to Say No to Drugs! A Parent/Child Manual for the Protection of Children; Alan Garner; Tom Doherty Associates; New York; 1987

Quotations from
Drug Users
and Counselors

(With more activities for children)

Quotations from Drug Users and Counselors

The following pages have quotations from drug users and professionals who work with them. They are grouped by subject matter and have activities for each section.

Quotations marked with * were taken from *Designer Drugs,* © 1986, by M.M. Kirsch, CompCare Publishers.

Other quotations were contributed by Community Care Network, Behavioral Systems Southwest, Phoenix Memorial Hospital, and the man on the street. The author wishes to thank all of them for their permission to share these quotations with you.

WHO USES DRUGS?

DRUG USE ISN'T JUST BY KIDS OR OLD HIPPIES. IT AFFECTS ALL LEVELS AND RACES OF PEOPLE.

Kids who "...did not become compulsive until they tried (a drug), tripling and quadrupling their use, missing school, stealing from their parents and lying to their friends...kids from upper-middle class families...with no history of addiction or psychiatric illness. They were in the top half of their class, college bound and they were addicted almost instantaneously. They were rendered completely dysfunctional by (a drug) in a two or three month period."*

"I've seen people from 9-80. They were from poor, middle, and upper class."

"It's all ages and levels, from little kids to grandmas, rich and poor alike."

"Most of the people I seen doing drugs were just kids when they started. But some were real old and they started anyway."

"I know of real successful people—professionals who were doing real well. They've lost it all—career, home, family, everything. Just like I did."

ACTIVITIES

1. Why do you think the drug problem is affecting all levels and races of people?

2. Find out about the history of drug use. It didn't start with the young people of the 60's.

3. Act out a conversation between two people on drugs who are opposites somehow, like a grandpa and his granddaughter, or a rich person and a poor person.

4. Write a story about a UFO coming to earth and what happens when the aliens see all different types of people smoking, drinking, and doing drugs.

WHY DO PEOPLE START USING DRUGS?

"I didn't really have any friends, and I thought this would help me fit in. I was tired of being lonely."

"I never had any confidence. I thought drugs would make me feel attractive and appealing."

"When I had drugs, kids would call me. That made me think I was important. But they just wanted my drugs."

"All my friends did drugs. They talked me into it. Once I tried it, it was all downhill."

"I was trying to escape from myself. I wanted to feel like a different person."

"Time stopped. I like feeling real far away from everything."

ACTIVITIES

1. *Weekly Reader's* survey found that the main reasons kids try drugs is to fit in, to feel older, and to have a good time. Brainstorm all the ways kids can fit in, feel older, and have a good time without substance abuse.

2. Make puppets and have a puppet show. Have the puppets discuss all the reasons kids start taking drugs, and what they could do instead.

3. Think about all the reasons kids try drugs. Discuss ways to meet these needs and have fun without drugs.

4. Pretend you are one of the people who wrote one of the quotes you just read. Write a letter to Ann Landers, explaining your problems and how you feel. Trade letters with someone else. Pretend you are Ann Landers and write an answer to the letter you have.

5. Collect advertisements that promote tobacco, alcohol, and drugs (including medicinal drugs) and also those that are against substance abuse. Which did you find more of? Study the ads. What do they promise you?

HOW ALCOHOL AND DRUGS
AFFECT PEOPLE SOCIALLY

"All I wanted to do was (drugs)...I had a habit that was costing me $1,500 to $1,800 a month...I had to see the jailhouse door slammed shut...I had to see my family shy away from me, the wife I doubt I could live without grow disgusted, the mother and father I love and respect grow ashamed. I had to see...close friends go through the same deterioration...their talents blowing away."*

"Our friends...think nobody can tell they are high...They glide around like Mr. and Mrs. Perfect, real quiet, real mellow...if you're short cash...you can ask 'em for the extra bucks and they'll never remember loaning it to you!"*

"Drug use affects relationships with your family, friends, and everyone. Your life revolves around drugs. Everything else, including people, is secondary. Your family disintegrates."

"My friends and I blew $200 in just an hour. We stole the money from my parents."

"Drug addiction leads to ostracism by all but your drug addicted friends. No one else wants anything to do with you anymore."

"Antisocial behavior becomes the norm."

"I destroyed my family and myself."

"I started to lie, cheat, and steal. I lost my job, friends, and loved ones."

"I've lost everything I ever owned, split up relationships, alienated my family and friends, and gone to prison because of drugs."

ACTIVITIES

1. Plan what you could do for fun with two friends and $200 if you didn't need drugs.

2. Pick one of the quotations and pretend you are the person it's about. Make up a story about what life is like for you.

3. Make a picture that illustrates some of the social effects drugs can have on kids.

4. Write a soap opera about someone on drugs.

WHEN PEOPLE TRY TO TALK YOU INTO USING ALCOHOL OR DRUGS, THEY TELL YOU HOW GREAT IT IS. HERE'S WHAT HAPPENS WHEN IT'S NOT SO GOOD.

"I can only think of one word. Frightening."

"I was SICK. I puked all night. I was seeing double. I hated it."

"It was depressing. Really depressing. I felt completely empty and worthless. I felt guilty. I just wanted to cry."

"I felt trapped. I just sat and stared at my hands the whole time. I wondered what hands were for."

"It's like life as you know it is over, but you're not dead."

"My first time was terrible. I couldn't stand still. My heart was racing so fast I thought I'd die for sure. But when it was over, I just made up excuses why it was bad, and I did it again the next time my friends did."

"I thought I was smart. If it got really bad, I'd just look at my watch. I knew it would wear off in a couple hours. I'd just look at my watch, and I knew I'd be OK. But this one time, I looked at my watch, and I couldn't tell time. I couldn't even see the hands or remember when I took the stuff. I was scared to death. I thought I was dying."

"I hated how I felt. The food looked sickening. I thought everyone at the party was watching me, that they had poisoned me just to watch me die. It wasn't the way I thought it would be, but I did it again at the next party."

ACTIVITIES

1. Talk about an experience you thought would be good, but it wasn't.

2. Why do you think these people keep doing drugs after they've had bad experiences?

3. Create your own comic strip characters. Make a children's comic book about the characters' experiences with alcohol and drugs.

111

AT BEST, DRUGS ARE RISKY. THERE'S NO SUCH THING AS SAFE OR RESPONSIBLE DRUG USE.

"The ultimate risk is death. Other than that, there is physical, mental, and emotional impairment. The user suffers. Development stops when drug use begins."

"You can die. Or wish you had. I've had so many bad trips, I've lost count."

"People think it's so great to get high — but what they call high is the effects of being poisoned. That's part of the trip. It doesn't kill too many people, but it's poison, none the less. And it does permanent brain damage."

"Lots of people have died from the chemists' synthetic drugs. But the chemists keep making the stuff, and people keep buying it. Most of them don't have any idea what they're getting. They all say they'd know the difference, but they don't."

"Young people are getting something like Parkinson's disease. And there's no cure. Just a hospital bed. And no more parties."

"Since you don't know what you're getting, you don't know how much to use. If it usually takes five hits, then you do five hits. But maybe this time, you got a synthetic that 5000 times stronger, and not cut very much. That makes it your last one."

"You risk your health. And you risk arrest and imprisonment."

"You never know who has AIDS. They don't want to tell you, but they'll be glad to share needles with you."

"There's lots of financial and legal risks, even if you don't care about your health."

ACTIVITIES

1. Brainstorm all the risks a person takes for each category: 1) drinking, 2) smoking, and 3) doing drugs. Comment on the severity and permanence of each category. (One thing that isn't a risk is brain damage. It's guaranteed. The non-mature, growing brain of kids and teenagers is permanently damaged by all three substances.)

2. Which, if any, of these risks are you willing to take? Explain the reasons for your answer.

3. Write a poem or a song about the risks of drug use.

4. At first, people have fun with tobacco, alcohol, and drugs, but it is risky. Later, it is not fun at all. What can you do for fun that won't hurt you?

5. Have kids write an editorial to their local newspaper about the risks of substance abuse.

WITH DRUGS, YOU DON'T EVEN KNOW WHAT YOU'RE GETTING

An arrested manufacturer of (a synthetic drug) was asked if a user could tell the difference between the synthetic and the real thing. He said, "No." When asked what he would advise users to do, he smiled and said, "Just say no."*

"The seller is not required to label his/her product. You can only be sure by using it—if you survive."

"You never know. I always wait until someone else takes a hit first. If they're OK, then I do mine."

"The death rate is very high from things being used to grow, cut, or dilute drugs. Sometimes the dealers just try to make money by selling something that looks like drugs. Sometimes it's even poisonous."

"Most people don't know what they're really getting, but they take it anyway."

"People don't consider the risk. Getting high is all that matters. They don't think about the bad stuff that put the other guy in the hospital for the rest of his life."

"Kids spend lots of money to buy drugs, and what they sometimes get is Raid, powdered light bulbs, cooking spices, or worse."

ACTIVITIES

1. Discuss all the reasons why people would take drugs when it's impossible to identify what they're getting.

2. Find out at what ages young children usually die from accidental poisoning. Find out the number of people who die from poisoning by taking drugs. Most eight- year-olds won't eat something if they don't know what it is. Why do you think people do it when they are older, and are supposed to be smarter?

3. Make a list of all the white powders found in your house. How many of them would you eat? If someone handed you a bag of white powder, and all they would tell you is, "I found it in my house," would you make brownies with it?

SPECIAL ACTIVITY TO BE PLANNED
BY AN ADULT

Prepare baggies of white powders commonly found in the home. Number the baggies and then see if the kids can identify each powder. DON'T USE ANYTHING POISONOUS, but for the sake of the lesson, tell them that one bag has rat poison in it. (Watch and see if anyone tries tasting the powders in their attempts to identify each one! Discuss why no one tasted the powders.)

The next day, give them a list of the contents, without saying which bag has which. Let them try again. Let them have the list to study and try again the third day.

The moral of the story is: if they can't even identify common household powders 100% accurately, how will they know what they are getting from a drug dealer or whether a synthetic drug was accurately produced? Even the drug dealers say they can't tell, and admit people don't know what they're getting.

Suggested white powders:

baking powder	laundry soap
baking soda	baby powder
flour	talcum powder
powdered sugar	powdered milk
granulated sugar	instant potato mix
salt	instant baby cereal
corn starch	cake mix
pancake mix	

IF YOU EVER WANT TO SEE
YOUR BRAIN ALIVE AGAIN...

"The very first time I did (drugs), it literally brought me to my knees...But it's just that one time. I spent three months (doing drugs) always doing more and more trying to get that same first rush again...I quit after (doing it) one weekend from 10 A.M. Saturday until 1 P.M. the next day non-stop. It hit me all of a sudden what a scumbag I'd become. Sleeping all day and (doing drugs) all night. It's the same feeling you get buying on credit. You experience this reward without deserving it. I had no control in my life and business. I was a scumbag."*

"Anyone that's been through the (drug) game pretty much knows you only get high for the first six days (months?)...and that's the only high you get. After that, you're paying dearly to just stay well. You never get high again."*

(This happens because the user will never again have the same number of neurotransmitters in his brain. They start burning out after the first "rush." No pleasurable experience will ever be what it used to be. The damage is permanent from the first usage.)

"I haven't touched that stuff in over a year, but I still get tripped out sometimes. It's a real pain. The doctor says the stuff's stored in my brain, and this could keep happening for years. I wish I'd never done it even once."

"It killed my brain cells." (The brain does not feel pain, so you can't tell it's being damaged until you see the loss of some function — and then it's too late.)

"You become as stupid as a rock. I've seen my friends go from smart to stupid."

"You want to know what it does to your thinking? Well, when my friend ODed (overdosed), everyone said, 'Hey, that must be really good stuff.' They went to the dealer for more, and he sold it all. That's how good you can think when you do drugs."

ACTIVITIES

1. Make a list of all the things you couldn't do very well if your brain was damaged.

2. How do you think people feel about themselves if they do things to damage their own brain? Pretend you were their counselor. What would you want them to learn?

3. Make a crossword puzzle about all the disadvantages of having a drug damaged brain.

LONG TERM DANGERS

"A little known problem that is rapidly growing is PDIS—Post-Drug Impairment Syndrome. Three to five million of today's kids will grow up unable to handle money, keep a job, or stay in one place. They will be unable to form normal emotional bonds. We may have to take care of these kids for their whole lives. Just getting the kids off drugs doesn't mean everything is going to be ok. Some damage can be permanent."

"The nervous system is not fully developed during the teen-age years. This makes it especially susceptible to damage from drug use. Teenagers can do as much damage to their brains in six months of drug use as an adult does in ten years of heavy drinking. The areas most likely to be affected are memory, comprehension, problem solving, decision making, and the ability to foresee probable consequences. So the more drugs kids use, the more certain they are that 'It won't happen to me.'!"

"Your development stops when you start drugs. You risk never maturing beyond the level you are now. As a 10 or 12 year old, you might think you're pretty cool, but do you think you want to act like a 10 or 12 year old when you're 20, 40 or 60?"

"Some of the risks include impaired emotional development. Some of these kids will never be able to bond normally or form permanent relationships. Not only will that mean many divorces or split relationships, think about the children they will have. Imagine the increase in child abuse and neglect when people who are unable to form emotional bonds try to raise children. And most of them will be trying to do it without the partner that produced the children."

"The brain has growth spurts at approximately ages two, six, ten, and fourteen. The growth spurt lasts from six months to two years. If kids take drugs during the time period in which the brain is trying to have a growth spurt, serious damage can be done. The kids are giving themselves a frontal lobotomy."

ACTIVITIES

1. For one day, have the kids write down how often and in what situations, they use the following skills: memory, comprehen-

119

sion, problem solving, decision making, and the ability to foresee probable consequences. Tell them to write down the decisions they made. Then discuss how the decisions might have
been different if they had less skill in each of the areas.

2. Write a comedy about a group of adults who still act like children because of their drug abuse.

3. Pretend you are the child of someone who is damaged by drug
use and can't really love them or anyone else. Discuss or act out
a short play to show what that life would be like, both for the
parent and the child.

4. Have kids collect magazine pictures of things they can do if they
aren't damaged by drugs.

DRUG PROBLEMS—THOUGHTS OF SUICIDE

"I think about killing myself. I just can't take it anymore."

"I looked at the knife and thought how easy it would be. I made a few cuts and smeared the blood all over the house. I thought I was in a murder movie, only I was the murderer and the victim. I thought about being in the headlines. But my dad came home and took me to the hospital before I was done."

"When I drive, sometimes I think 'All it would take would be to just go a little left of center.' Then it would be over. It could look like an accident and my parents would never know. I feel so guilty about everything I've done."

"I have lots of sleeping pills. I think about taking them. If it gets any worse, I will."

"I've tried running away. I've hitched all over the country. The more scared I get, the more I run. Maybe I'll get picked up by a murderer so someone who's happy won't get wasted. Then I will have at least done something good with my life."

"The only thing that stops me is I can't change my mind later. Maybe if I hang on, it'll get better. If I kill myself, I don't get another chance."

ACTIVITIES

1. Why do you think people want to kill themselves? What would you recommend these people do?

2. How do the friends and family feel when someone kills himself?

3. Write all the things you would miss if you killed yourself. How many of these would you miss out on anyway if you got involved with drugs?

INSTANT DEATH — AND SOMETIMES YOU DON'T EVEN GET HIGH FIRST

"At one of the funerals for the hypes that overdosed, one of the dealers attended. A friend of the hype who died, an addict himself, accosted the dealer at the funeral and accused him of selling bad (drugs). The dealer said it was great stuff and gave the hype a free sample. They found him dead in his car."*

"I personally know of five instances of overdose. These were close friends who either did too much of one drug or mixed drugs together."

"I have known at least a dozen people to die from overdoses."

"My friend was found with the needle still in her arm. It was that fast."

"He always said it wouldn't happen to him. He knew his drugs. That's what he always said."

"I've known several people to die from drugs. I'm sure it was synthetics. The last one, she spent $3,000 a month on the stuff, she'd seen a lot of it, she was sure she knew what she was getting because she'd been doing it for twenty years."

ACTIVITIES

1. Instant death can happen the first time a person tries drugs. What do you think about people's advice to just use drugs responsibly, the same as adults who might have one or two beers occasionally?

2. If someone had a bowl of candy, but told you one piece had poison in it, would you help yourself to some candy? Why do you think people are willing to play Russian Roulette with drugs?

3. Use a paper scroll and a box to make a TV commercial about drugs and the risk of instant death.

PEOPLE ARE QUITTING

"...they all know they can die from an overdose and they all know they can die from being killed by some pusher but they've never been threatened with such a hideous disease as AIDS...It wasn't overnight that these people stopped using. A lot of things happened. There were several deaths in the group. They saw four, five, six people that were in their social life die. In one case, one man in the group has been ill and it might be the beginning of AIDS...it's scary. And it's been very, very frightening."*

"People quit when it's no longer a need. They work on their problems so they don't need drugs to escape."

"They get tired of hiding from themselves."

"People get tired of waking up on the rug."

"I gave up drugs because I was tired of the lifestyle and I outgrew them."

"I'm quitting because I'm tired of destroying my life."

"They're sick of being sick."

"I was tired of spending $600 a day. I started thinking what else I could do. So I went to the drug clinic."

"I was tired of coughing up all this black — —."

"Who wants to risk hepatitis or AIDS?"

ACTIVITIES

1. It's not easy to quit drugs, especially after the point of addiction. Discuss all the reasons people would want to quit.

2. What would you do with $600 a day if you didn't need to spend it on drugs?

3. Get a large piece of heavy cardboard. Make a mosaic, using seeds, dried beans, macaroni, shredded paper, or whatever. Have the poster tell why people are quitting drugs.

4. Write a poem or song about why people are quitting.

WHAT ADVICE WOULD YOU GIVE TO KIDS?

"Don't use that first time. Don't associate with people who do drugs."

"Don't be afraid to be yourself. If you are content being yourself, you don't have a desire to use drugs."

"Say no to drugs. ALL DRUGS."

"STAY AWAY! I'm twenty years behind where I should be because of the choices I've made."

"Drugs will destroy your life!"

"Remember, no one forces you to experiment with drugs. It's your decision and all the problems will be your responsibility."

"If you even think about doing drugs, find someone to talk to who can help you. Promise yourself you'll do that before you even try anything once."

"Maybe your parents did do drugs when they were kids and it didn't seem to hurt them. But the drug scene is much riskier now. The marijuana is stronger. There's synthetics. The drugs aren't pure. It just isn't worth the risk."

"You think you can do drugs and not get hurt. But do you really want to take the chance?"

ACTIVITIES

1. Have the kids discuss their opinion of this advice to kids.

2. Discuss the advice your family would give to kids.

3. Make a picture of the one thing that you think is most important for kids to remember so they won't do drugs.

WHAT ADVICE WOULD YOU GIVE
TO PARENTS?

"Talk to your children early. Keep them informed. Make drugs sound like the worst kind of poison or sin. Keep them away from users. Watch how you treat your kids, such as parenting problems."

"Allow your children to be themselves, that it's OK to be you."

"Tell your kids 'I love you' and to leave drugs alone."

"If you think there's even a remote chance your kids are doing drugs, go see a counselor."

"Set a good example for your children. They are our next presidents and doctors."

"Listen to your children. Talk to them."

"Be honest with your kids, both about your feelings about drugs, and your knowledge of drugs. In most cases, your kids will be honest with you."

"Read parenting books and take classes. You only get one chance to raise your kids. Learn all you can so you can do the best you can. Then you won't have to wish you had."

"Spend time with your kids. Even if you work two jobs and go to school, they need you just as much as if you were home all day. Find the time, somehow."

"Don't let your kids watch all that crap on TV. Take them to the library or buy them a horse. Get them busy enjoying real life so they don't need to escape."

ACTIVITIES

1. Discuss everyone's reactions to this advice to parents. Do you agree with all, some, or none of it?

2. Discuss what everyone thinks the perfect parents would be like.

3. Talk about your own family—what you are happy with and what you wish was different.

4. Write down the names of movies and TV shows that promote tobacco, alcohol, and drugs and also those that are against sub-

stance abuse. Which did you find more of? Based on this information, should parents let kids watch whatever they want? What advice would you give parents about kids, TV, and movies?

5. Write a letter of advice to parents about how to raise happy kids who don't need drugs.

WHOSE RESPONSIBILITY IS IT?

"Realistically, it is impossible to protect a person who will not take the responsibility for protecting himself. In England, where heroin addicts are given sterile opiates and syringes, the incidence of hepatitis and bloodstream infections matches ours...Addicts tend to be careless or uncaring about these matters...Those who inject, smoke or swallow dubious substances have no self-esteem, no concept of future consequences, are extremely immature or self-destructive."*

ACTIVITIES

1. Discuss how you feel about the previous quotation. What do you think the government should do to protect people? Do you think it's the government's job to take care of people or should people be responsible for themselves? Remember, tax dollars pay the bill.

2. Research and collect articles on what our government (and others) is doing to fight drugs.

3. If you had a magic wand that was good for one wish, how would you use it to prevent substance abuse? (No fair wishing for more wishes!)

The Goal

Characteristics of Drug-Free Children

(No one has all these characteristics — but the more your child has, the better his chances.)

1. The kids have high esteem.

2. The kids feel valued and secure in the family.

3. The kids feel listened to — they know their opinion is important, even if they didn't get their way.

4. The kids know they are accepted, even if they aren't able to do great in school, sports, or social situations.

5. The kids have a normal frustration tolerance. They don't expect to get everything they want, they don't expect to get things for nothing, and they don't expect everything to be easy.

6. The kids are able to take "no" for an answer, and they know their parents mean what they say.

7. The kids are balanced in being considerate of others and themselves.

8. The kids have many interests, and don't watch a lot of TV.

9. The kids have a low level of stress in their lives.

10. The kids have a limited amount of money.

11. The kids are capable of independent thinking and are not at risk for being talked into things.

12. The kids have adequate social skills for making friends and getting along.

13. The kids have good problem solving and decision making skills.

14. The kids have a strong belief system.

15. The kids invite their friends home.

Characteristics of the Homes of Drug-Free Children

1. The family and the marriage come first, the kids are important, but not put before the marriage.

2. The family has fun together.

3. The family eats together.

4. The family works together.

5. Family members feel appreciated.

6. The emphasis is on positive accomplishments.

7. Parents "practice what they preach" and are good role models in all areas.

8. The family has good communication skills.

9. The family is adaptable in meeting everyone's needs.

10. There is a commitment to spend the time and energy to solve problems.

11. The parents are reasonable and consistent in discipline. The kids know the parents mean what they say.

12. While there is strong family bonding, there is also a healthy amount of separateness and outside interests.

13. The parents have reasonable, positive expectations which the children live up to.

14. Parents are aware of their children's activities and supervise when it's appropriate.

15. Parents are aware of how much money the kids have, and how they spend it.

16. Differences are acceptable and children are encouraged to think independently.

17. The parents set a good example in problem solving and in dealing with a crisis.

18. The parents do not rescue the kids from the consequences of their behavior.

Necessary Ingredients for a Drug-Free Community

1. There must be a commitment to a drug-free environment.

2. People need an awareness of the facts about drugs and alcohol.

3. The community needs a tough, clear, consistently enforced anti-drug policy.

4. The community, schools, and family must support these policies whole-heartedly and make it clear that drug-related behavior will not be tolerated.

5. The formation of parent groups, peer groups, and school groups is important for providing support and positive attention to saying NO.

6. Parents need to be involved with the schools and their children's education.

7. Parents need to plan and chaperon no drug/no alcohol activities at home, church, school, or other organizations.

8. People need to be aware of and write letters regarding legislative action related to drugs and alcohol.

Drug Information

Drug-Related Statistics

Of junior and senior high students who experiment with drugs, one out of five becomes addicted.

A Weekly Reader survey found one in four fourth graders feel "some" or "a lot" of pressure to try cocaine, 36% feel pressure to try alcohol, and 41% are pressured to use tobacco.

By age 18, the average person has seen about 180,000 "ads" (scenes in movies, song lyrics, etc.) that make tobacco, drugs, and alcohol look appealing.

80% of drinking parents have drinking children. 70% of non-drinking parents have non-drinking children.

90% of today's young people try alcohol and drugs before they graduate from high school. 60% of those who have tried them use them regularly each week.

In the general population, one out of ten reaches addiction. That averages two or three children per classroom who are headed for serious trouble with drugs.

One out of every three high school students has been high or drunk, and two out of three have tried pot. In a classroom of thirty, that's ten who have been high or drunk, and twenty who have tried pot.

In most big cities, 60% of high school seniors use drugs two or three times a week, and almost one in four are stoned most of the time. And the small towns and rural areas are following close behind.

Most of the teens on drugs say they get high every morning before school.

Most kids start trying drugs in fifth or sixth grade.

The percentage of kids using marijuana has gone from 4% to over 50% in the past ten years.

Most of the drugs kids have, they buy and use in school.

15-25% of high school seniors use drugs "most of the time."

Kids who use drugs say they can go to a strange city and get any drug they want within 30 minutes.

Since Southland Corporation decided to stop selling rolling papers in their 7-11 stores, they lose $7,000,000 every year in their annual profit.

Drug use has increased 1000-3000% since the early 1960's.

Kids who use drugs have lower grades, have more problems with delinquency, commit more murders, and are more likely to commit suicide.

There has been a 60% increase in youth suicides over the past ten years.

Death rates have gone down in every age group, except 14-24. The main cause is alcohol and drug related suicides, traffic accidents, and overdose.

Americans consume 60% of the world supply of illegal drugs.

The number of 13 year olds who have used marijuana has increased 1500% in the last thirty-five years.

Half of the people admitted to federally funded drug treatment centers started smoking marijuana at age 14 or younger.

Smoking today's marijuana causes more lung damage, in a shorter time, than cigarette smoking.

There are more teenage drug users in the U.S. than in any other industrialized country.

Our drug problem is ten times greater than Japan's. 61% of high school seniors have tried drugs. 26% claim to have used marijuana at least once in the last thirty days (approximately one out of four — or an average of six or seven per classroom). 13% have used cocaine (approximately one out of seven or eight — or an average of three or four per classroom).

One out of every six 13-year-olds has tried marijuana. That's an average of four or five students in every seventh or eighth grade classroom.

A 2% content of THC (the main psychoactive ingredient in marijuana) can cause psychological damage. Most of today's marijuana has 4 to 6% THC. Ten years ago, most marijuana had less than 1% THC, often as little as 3/10%.

Alcohol is the favorite drug of students.

Alcohol is the number one cause of all accidents, especially car accidents.

Teenagers can do as much damage to their brains in six months of drug use as an adult does in ten years of heavy drinking. This is because the nervous system is not fully developed until after the teenage years. This makes it especially susceptible to damage from drug use. The areas most likely to be affected are memory, comprehension, problem solving, decision making, and the ability to foresee probable consequences. So the more drugs kids use, the more sure they honestly feel "It won't happen to me."!

Signs of Drug Use

During the first two stages of drug abuse, unless you "catch them in the act," there probably will be no signs to indicate drug use. Young people work very hard to keep everything looking normal. And they certainly aren't going to do it in front of you! At stage three, however, this becomes a losing battle and you will see one, two, and then increasingly more signs. If you *only* see one or two of the harmless symptoms, i.e., your child decides to quit bowling, and asks to borrow 5 dollars, don't panic! It's the total picture, and the increasing problems that mean you already have a very serious problem that can only be solved with professional help.

If you are a professional, you still need outside help. Many drug counselors have found their own kids on drugs. They said it was their experience that made them think they could handle it, and delayed getting the outside help they desperately needed. No matter how much expertise you have, you can't see the picture if you're in the frame.

If you are a teacher, being the kid's buddy won't help. He needs professional help, and if possible, to be involved in family counseling.

Here are warning signals to put you on "red alert."

PHYSICAL CLUES

1. Decrease in personal hygiene and dress standards, drastic change in hair style
2. Tobacco smell
3. Eyes red, dilated, contracted, frequent use of eye drops
4. Sudden constant runny nose
5. Eating extremes, unexplained weight loss
6. Chronic cough
7. Chest pains
8. Dulled speech and expression
9. Problems sleeping, or sleeping a lot
10. Menstrual irregularity
11. Poor health
12. Acting intoxicated
13. Lack of control of eye movements
14. Unusually and unexplainably pale
15. Wearing sunglasses more than normal
16. Frequently sick in the morning, OK by noon
17. Physical development abnormally slow or stopped altogether
18. Little energy

BEHAVIORAL CLUES

1. Sudden discipline problems
2. Withdraws into room
3. Stays away from home
4. Coming home later and later
5. Borrowing money more frequently
6. Stealing
7. Whispering on the phone
8. Stops making eye contact
9. Avoids the family
10. Lying
11. Breaking rules
12. Swearing at you
13. Destroying or damaging property in anger
14. Increase in number of arguments
15. Over-reacts

ATTITUDE CLUES

1. Caring less about everything—little enthusiasm or motivation
2. Negative change in attitude, argumentative, irritable, sarcastic
3. Moodiness, anxiety, hostile, irritable
4. Loneliness, depression, overly sensitive
5. Needs instant gratification

SCHOOL-RELATED CLUES

1. Skipping school, declining grades
2. Sudden discipline problems
3. Problems with concentration, attention span, memory
4. Change in friends to "less desirables"
5. Drug oriented graffiti, decals, etc. on notebooks or book covers
6. Frequently late for school
7. Falls asleep in class
8. Always has an excuse for whatever the problem is
9. No interest in school activities
10. Tries to get parents to take his side against teachers

SOCIAL CLUES

1. Sudden change of friends
2. Stops bringing friends home
3. Weird-looking friends
4. Increasingly more concerned with self and less concerned with others
5. Radical change in beliefs, values, ideals

STRONG INDICATORS — GET PROFESSIONAL HELP!

1. Finding drugs in the kid's possession
2. Loss of interest in most old favorite activities for no obvious reason
3. Distorted sense of time
4. Decrease in memory, attention span, and/or judgment

5. Paranoia
6. Room looks strange—drug oriented graffiti, decals, posters, etc.
7. Drug paraphernalia
8. Use of incense, breath fresheners, room deodorizers to cover smell of pot

Stages of Drug Use

No one consciously decides, "I think I'll be a drug addict when I grow up, or an alcoholic, or maybe I'll die of lung cancer." This is one of the reasons teaching the horrors of addiction is ineffective — just as teaching about lung cancer and alcoholism doesn't keep anyone from trying tobacco or alcohol the first time. What children must be aware of is that all of these substances can become like a downhill sled. Once you get started, it can be very hard to stop before you reach the bottom.

STAGE 1

A child usually first experiments with cigarettes, alcohol, and then other drugs (usually marijuana) in a social setting. Friends say, "Try it, you'll like it," so he does. Then they say, "You'll like it after you get used to it." So he keeps trying it.

At this stage, the person is only experimenting when it's convenient, usually on weekends. He's not buying his own yet. He finds it easy to get drunk or high, and it feels good. It also meets his need to impress, to be liked, to feel included.

At this stage, the person acts normal, and you would never know unless you caught him in the act.

STAGE 2

At this stage, the person begins seeking alcohol and/or drugs and begins buying his own. He starts using more for two reasons: his tolerance is increasing so he needs greater amounts to feel the same, and as the guilt increases, he takes more so he can escape the guilty feelings.

The person learns that alcohol and/or drugs make him feel good immediately, problems seem to vanish, and it works every time. He believes he'll never get caught or have a problem.

At the onset of stage 2, the person is using alcohol and/or drugs most weekends and some school days. The person still wants approval from family and school. He works hard to look normal and maintain his other interests.

Towards the end of stage 2, he is using drugs almost every day. He begins to plan his life and friends around his habit. As he gets used to marijuana and alcohol, he starts to try other drugs. He could start to lie, and in some cases, may even steal from his family to supplement his allowance and job. His new habits are getting expensive.

As stage 2 progresses, the individual alternates periods of social withdrawal (spends a lot of time alone in his room, rock music blasting) with being aggressive and angry (tantrums and bad language). His motivation declines. His former hobbies and interests seem to be just too much trouble and cut into his drug time. For example, feeling good from drugs is a whole lot easier than the work required to feel good as an athlete. He begins to get high when he's alone, and not just with friends. Alcohol and/or drugs are not just recreational anymore—they're needed to cope with everyday life, which he denies to himself. Teachers and parents feel there is a minor problem, probably "just a stage." As it gets increasingly difficult to maintain two lifestyles, alcohol and/or drug use increases even more.

STAGE 3

In stage 3, the use is almost daily. Being high is the number one thing in life. Drugs are used to feel good and to avoid feeling bad. As the person loses skill in dealing with everyday stress, frustration, disappointment, and challenges, the drug use further increases as a false way of coping. Harder drugs are used, in addition to alcohol and marijuana, in an attempt to have more fun at parties.

Most of the time, the person gets high alone. His old friends have been entirely replaced by druggies, and he no longer attempts to appear innocent himself. He begins to skip school and starts getting failing grades. He starts stealing from friends and strangers, in addition to selling drugs, to support his habit. This increases the feelings of guilt, which further increases the usage of drugs.

The person develops a constant cough, red eyes, sore throat, bronchitis, and fatigue. He feels depression each time he comes down from a high. He is verbally and/or physically abusive to his family.

At the end of stage 3, he takes drugs to escape the pain of the drugs. He thinks everyone else feels good from drugs, so he must be going crazy. He thinks about suicide. He loses control. He has legal problems. He can't complete tasks. His attention span is incredibly short. He can't think or concentrate, nor can he talk right. He loses his job and quits school (if he wasn't expelled already). He gets caught for possession and/or dealing with drugs. He runs away and is promiscuous. He leaves his drug paraphernalia in plain sight — no longer attempting to conceal his habit.

STAGE 4

At stage 4, the person uses drugs all the time in an attempt to just feel normal. Feeling good is a lost cause. He hurts, but he can't stop. He starts to "shoot up" to save time. His eyes are glazed, he's losing weight, his memory is shot, he's coughing, has chronic emotional pain, and frequent thoughts of suicide. He can no longer tell what is acceptable or unacceptable behavior. At this stage, many kids (both girls and now boys, too) go into prostitution as the easiest way to support their drug needs. The risk of AIDS is obvious. The slang to describe this zombie-like condition is "burnout" or "wasted."

Drugs have become a terminal disease. Drug related deaths include suicides, accidents, murder, cardiac arrest, kidney and liver failure, stroke, respiratory failure, and lung cancer, to name just a few.

ACTIVITIES FOR THE STAGES OF DRUG USE

1. Read these stages to the kids. Discuss how they feel about what you just read. Do they think it's true? Why do they think some people never try drugs at all, others try and quit, and still others proceed to stage 4?

2. Ask the kids to write twenty things they love to do. Put 1, 2, 3, or 4 by each one to show at what stage they would probably be unable to do it if they decided to do drugs. Drugs cost a lot of money and take up a lot of time. They can only spend their money once, and every hour spent on drugs is not available for other interests. Their brain is damaged, and as their health deteriorates, they are physically able to do less.

3. Write a diary of or about someone progressing from considering just trying drugs once, through stage four.

4. Make a notebook of drug articles.

Types of Drugs

There are basically four kinds of drugs.

Stimulants are commonly called uppers. They increase the pulse rate and raise blood pressure.

Depressants are known as downers. They slow down the brain and the nervous system.

Hallucinogens cause changes in the brain's perceptions, resulting in illusions and hallucinations. Sensory input is distorted, so the person thinks he hears colors and sees sounds.

Narcotics are commonly called painkillers, as they keep the person from experiencing their pain (which is still there, but the message is not received by the brain).

RECOMMENDED READING

10 Startling New Facts About Brain Damage and Marijuana; David Goodman; D.G. Futurist Publications; Culver City, California; 1983

Designer Drugs; M.M.Kirsch; CompCare Publications; Minneapolis, Minnesota; 1986

"Growth Spurts During Brain Development" Herman Epstein; Chapter 10, *Education and the Brain;* University of Chicago Press; 1979

Not My Kid: A Parent's Guide to Kids and Drugs; Beth Polson & Miller Newton; Avon Books; New York, New York; 1984

Post-Drug Impairment Syndrome (PDIS); Forrest S. Tennant; Veract, Inc.; West Covina, California; 1985

Raising Drug-Free Kids in a Drug-Filled World; William Mack Perkins & Nancy McMurtrie-Perkins; Harper-Row; New York, New York; 1986

Names of Drugs

Here are some slang or pharmaceutical names for drugs. *This is not to be given to the children*—they don't need to learn about yet another drug they could try. (Teachers—in some states it is illegal to mention names of drugs the kids aren't already aware of!) This is only included for your information, so if you hear kids talking about something suspicious, you can look here to see if it is a drug they are discussing.

It can also be used to assess the kids' awareness of drugs. If you ask them to tell you or write down all the drugs they know about, you can look here to find out the real name for a slang term they might use. Of course, the slang changes constantly, and new substances are found to abuse, so this list will not be "all there is to abuse."

2,5-DMA—synthetic amphetamines and/or methamphetamines (hallucinogens)

25—lysergic acid diethylamide (LSD)

45 minute psychosis—dimethltryptamine (DMT)

714's—Quaaludes

a moon—peyote

A's—amphetamines

acid—lysergic acid diethylamide (LSD)

Acapulco Gold—marijuana

amidone—methadone

and blue's—a narcotic

angel dust — phencyclidine (PCP)

barbs — barbiturates

beans — amphetamines

bennies — amphetamines

Bernice — cocaine

Bernies — cocaine

bhang — marijuana

Big C — cocaine

big chief — peyote

Big D — lysergic acid diethylamide (LSD)

Big H — heroin

Big Harry — heroin

biscuit — Quaalude (methaqualone)

bitter — exempt preparations

black beauties — amphetamines

black tar — heroin

blow — cocaine

blue acid — lysergic acid diethylamide (LSD)

blue angels — amphetamines

blue birds — barbiturates

blue devils — barbiturates

blue heaven — lysergic acid diethylamide (LSD)

blue heavens — barbiturates

blue velvet — exempt preparations

blues — barbiturates

bolt — butyl nitrite (locker deodorant)

bombido — amphetamines

bombita — methamphetamine

boo — marijuana

boy — heroin

brown sugar — heroin

browns — amphetamines

bullet — isobutyl nitrite (locker deodorant)

bumblebees — amphetamines

bump — cocaine

Burese — cocaine

bush — marijuana

business man's special — dimethltryptamine (DMT)

butter flower — marijuana

buttons — mescaline, peyote

C — cocaine

caballo — heroin

'caine — cocaine

cactus — peyote, mescaline

candy — cocaine and other depressants

Carrie — cocaine

cartwheels — amphetamines

cecil — cocaine

China White — a synthetic heroin

cholly — cocaine

Christmas trees — barbiturates

'cid — lysergic acid diethylamide (LSD)

climax — isobutyl nitrite (locker deodorant)

coast to coast — amphetamines

cocaine — a narcotic

codeine — a narcotic

coke — cocaine

co-pilots — amphetamines

Corine — cocaine

crack — a form of cocaine

crank — methamphetamine, crystal meth

crystal — methamphetamine, amphetamines

crystal meth — methedrine or desoxyn
cube — morphine
cubes — lysergic acid diethylamide (LSD)
Demerol — meperidine
designer drugs — synthetic narcotics
dexies — amphetamines
Dilaudid — hydromorphone (a narcotic)
DOB — synthetic amphetamines and/or methamphetamines (hallucinogens)
doe — methamphetamine
Dolantol — meperidine
Dolophine — methadone
dollies — methadone
dolls — methadone
doobies — marijuana cigarettes
DOM — STP, synthetic amphetamines and/or methamphetamines (hallucinogens)
doojee — heroin
dope — marijuana or heroin
double trouble — barbiturates
DMP — dimethltryptamine (DMT)
dreamer — morphine
duige — heroin
dynamite — cocaine
dynamite & dolly — heroin
ecstasy — an amphetamine variant
emsel — morphine
eye openers — amphetamines
fentanyl — synthetic heroin

flake — cocaine
flasher — glue, chemicals, and aerosols
footballs — amphetamines
freebase rocks — crack, cocaine
gage — marijuana
ganga — marijuana
gas — glue, chemicals, and aerosols
giggles-smoke — marijuana
gin — cocaine
girl — cocaine
go-fast — methamphetamine
gold dust — cocaine
goof balls — a depressant, amphetamines
grass — marijuana
green dragon — lysergic acid diethylamide (LSD)
greenies — amphetamines
griffo — marijuana
H — heroin
hairy — heroin
half moon — peyote
happy dust — cocaine
hard stuff — morphine, heroin
Harry — heroin
has — marijuana
hashish — a stronger form of marijuana
hay — marijuana
hearts — amphetamines
heaven dust — cocaine
heavenly blue — lysergic acid diethylamide (LSD)
hemp — marijuana
herb — marijuana
heroin — a narcotic

hikori — peyote
hikuli — peyote
hocus — morphine
hog — phencyclidine (PCP)
horse — heroin
huatari — peyote
hydromorphone — a narcotic
Indian hay — marijuana
instant Zen — lysergic acid
    diethylamide (LSD)
Isonipecaine — meperidine
J — marijuana
jelly babies — amphetamines
jive — marijuana
joint — marijuana
joint sticks — marijuana
jolly beans — amphetamines
joy powder — heroin, cocaine
juice — alcoholic beverage
junk — heroin
kidstuff — glue, chemicals, and
    aerosols
killer weed — strong marijuana
    or marijuana with another
    drug added
LA turnabouts —
    amphetamines
lady — cocaine
laughing gas
lemmons — Quaalude
lemonade — heroin
licorice — exempt preparations
lid — marijuana
lid poppers — amphetamines
little D — hydromorphone
locker room — isobutyl nitrite
    (locker deodorant)
loco weed — marijuana
Lomotil — a narcotic

Lords — hydromorphone
loveboat — phencyclidine
    (PCP)
love weed — marijuana
lovely — phencyclidine (PCP)
lude — Quaaludes
M — morphine
MDA — methylenedioxy-
    amphetamine
MDM — synthetic
    amphetamines and/or
    methamphetamines
    (hallucinogens)
MDMA — synthetic
    amphetamines and/or
    methamphetamines
    (hallucinogens)
MPPP — synthetic heroin
MPTP — synthetic heroin
magic marshmallows —
    marijuana wrapped in a
    leaf and roasted
magic mushrooms —
    psilocybin (hallucinogen)
Mary Jane — marijuana
Mary Warner — marijuana
maui wowie — marijuana
melter — morphine
mendrex — methaqualone
mesc — peyote
mescal beans — peyote
mescal button — peyote
mescaline — an alkaloid from
    peyote cactus
meth — methamphetamine
methadone — a narcotic
methadose — methadone
Methedrine — methampheta-
    mine

microdot — lysergic acid diethylamide (LSD)
Miss Emma — morphine
Mohasky — marijuana
monkey — morphine
morf — morphine
morphie — morphine
morphine — a narcotic
morhpo — morphine
mu — marijuana
mud — heroin
muggles — marijuana
mushrooms — psilocybin (hallucinogen)
mutah — marijuana
nimbles — barbiturates
nimby — barbiturates
nose candy — cocaine
opium — a narcotic
oranges — amphetamines
P — peyote
PCE — synthetic phencyclidine (PCP, a hallucinogen)
PCP — phencyclidine (PCP)
PCPy — synthetic phencyclidine (PCP, a hallucinogen)
peace — STP
peace pill — phencyclidine (PCP)
PEPAP — synthetic heroin
Percodan — a narcotic
PG — exempt preparations
PO — exempt preparations
paradise — cocaine
peach pill — phencyclidine (PCP)
peaches — amphetamines
peanuts — other depressants

pearly gates — lysergic acid diethylamide (LSD)
pep pills — amphetamines and other stimulants
Pethidine — meperidine
phennies — barbiturates
pink ladies — barbiturates
pinks — barbiturates
PMA — synthetic amphetamines and/or methamphetamines (hallucinogens)
pod — marijuana
pop — phencyclidine (PCP)
poppers — amyl nitrite
pot — marijuana
purple haze — hallucinogen
purple hearts — amphetamines
psilocybin mushrooms — hallucinogen
Quaaludes — methaqualone
quad — Quaaludes
quay — Quaaludes
rainbow — amphetamines
rainbows — lysergic acid diethylamide (LSD)
red and blues — barbiturates
red birds — barbiturates
red devil — amphetamines
red devils — barbiturates
red dragon — lysergic acid diethylamide (LSD)
red water — exempt preparations
reds — barbiturates
reefers — marijuana
RJS — amphetamine
roach — marijuana
rock — crack or cocaine

roses — amphetamines
royal blue — lysergic acid diethylamide (LSD)
rush — amyl nitrite or butyl nitrite (locker deodorant)
sacred mushrooms — psilocybin (hallucinogen)
salt — heroin
sativa — marijuana
schmeek — heroin
schoolboy — codeine, cough syrup
seccy — barbiturates
seni — peyote
sens — high quality marijuana
serenity — STP
sheesh — hashish
shit — heroin
sinsemilla — marijuana
skag — heroin
sky-rockets — a stimulant
sleeping pills — other depressants
smack — heroin
smoke — marijuana
snappers — amyl nitrite
snow — heroin, cocaine
snowbirds — cocaine
soaps — Quaaludes
sopor — Quaaludes
speed — methamphetamine, amphetamine
speedball — cocaine
splash — methamphetamine
splim — marijuana
spray — glue, chemicals, and aerosols
Star dust — cocaine

STP — synthetic amphetamines and/or methamphetamines (hallucinogens)
straw — marijuana
stuff — heroin
sugar — lysergic acid diethylamide (LSD)
sugar cubes — lysergic acid diethylamide (LSD)
sugar lump — lysergic acid diethylamide (LSD)
supergrass — phencyclidine (PCP)
sweets — amphetamines
synthetic acid — STP
synthetic heroin — analogs of fentanyl
synthetic marijuana — phencyclidine (PCP)
T — a narcotic
tab — morphine
TCP — synthetic phencyclidine (PCP, a hallucinogen)
tea — marijuana, or sold as delta-9-THC (but is usually really PCP)
Texas tea — marijuana
THC — tetrahydrocannabinol (the psychoactive ingredient in marijuana)
the bad seed — peyote
the button — peyote
the Chief — lysergic acid diethylamide (LSD)
the Hawk — lysergic acid diethylamide (LSD)
the leaf — cocaine

thing – heroin
TMA – synthetic amphetamines and/or methamphetamines (hallucinogens)
tooies – barbiturates
tops – peyote
toot – cocaine
tranquillity – STP
truck drivers – amphetamines
unkie – morphine
uppers – amphetamines and other stimulants
ups – amphetamines
vitamin A – lysergic acid diethylamide (LSD)
vitamin Q – Quaaludes or methaqualone
wake ups – amphetamines
wedding bells – lysergic acid diethylamide (LSD)
weed – marijuana
whippets – the propellant in the aerosol spray can of whipped cream
white – cocaine
white girl – cocaine
white lightning – lysergic acid diethylamide (LSD)
white stuff – morphine, heroin
whites – amphetamines
wokowi – peyote
yellow jacket – amphetamines, barbiturates
yellows – barbiturates
Zen – lysergic acid diethylamide (LSD)

Glossary

This is for parent use only! It is not intended to be used to teach kids drug slang.

addiction—physiological and psychological need for a substance, whether it be alcohol, caffeine, tobacco, or drugs

amphetamine—a stimulant that affects the central nervous system to produce higher energy and reduces the desire to eat or sleep

base smoking—a way of using cocaine, by heating it and breathing the vapors

balloon—used to package drugs

blasted—to be intoxicated or very high

blow pages some dope—to smoke marijuana

bong—pipe used to smoke marijuana

bong hit—one inhalation from a bong

bowl—the part of the pipe the marijuana is put into, or that amount of marijuana a bowl will hold

brew—beer

bummer—a bad drug experience, or any bad experience

burn-out—a person who is intoxicated or high all the time

busted—getting caught

buzzed—being high through the use of alcohol or drugs

carburetor—a type of pipe used for smoking marijuana

clips — short for roach clips that are used to hold a marijuana cigarette when it's too short to hold by hand

cool — using drugs

cop — meaning to buy heroin

cop a buzz — to get high

cut — something used to dilute a drug

dealing — to sell drugs

designer drugs — synthetic drugs that try to produce the same effects as the real drugs

detox — short for detoxification, the removal of the drugs and their effects from the body

dime bag — $10 worth of marijuana

doobies — marijuana cigarettes

dope — for heroin or marijuana

downers — for drugs that depress the central nervous system

forensic labs — police labs

freak — someone who looks and acts like a drug user

freak-out — the way someone acts while having a bad drug experience

freebase — for a form of cocaine used in smoking

getting blitzed — getting high

getting lit — getting high

getting ripped — getting high

getting wasted — getting high

head — someone who has taken up the appearance and lifestyle of a drug user

heat — law enforcement

herb — marijuana

hit — a single dose or inhalation of a drug

huffing — inhaling gases to get high

hype — someone who shoots up cocaine

J — a marijuana cigarette

joint — a marijuana cigarette

junk — heroin

killer weed — strong marijuana or marijuana with another drug added

lid — a little more than an ounce of marijuana

line — a thin line of cocaine, put on a glass surface to be snorted

munchies — the craving for sweet or salty food that accompanies marijuana intoxication mushrooms — hallucinogenic mushrooms

narc — a policeman, or anyone who turns in drug users

nickel bag — $5 worth of marijuana

ounce — an ounce of cocaine or marijuana

OZ — ounce

papers — used to roll marijuana cigarettes

party — to get high

pharmies — prescribed drugs

pinwheel — a thin marijuana cigarette

pinned — intoxicated

pot — marijuana

power hitter — used to increase the effects of a marijuana cigarette

PWA — Person With AIDS

reefer — a marijuana cigarette

roach — the butt of the marijuana cigarette

roach clips — used to hold the marijuana cigarette when it gets too short to hold by hand

run — to be used very regularly

'script — for prescription drugs that can be used to get high

shoot up — injecting drugs with a needle

shot gun — blowing smoke from the marijuana cigarette directly into another user's mouth

shrooms — hallucinogenic mushrooms

smoke — slang, marijuana

snorting — to take a drug by sniffing into the nose

spent — slang, when there's nothing left of the marijuana but the ashes

spoon — used to melt drugs for injection

stash — slang, hidden drugs

step on — to dilute the drug with another substance to increase the quantity available to sell

stogie — a very big marijuana cigarette

stoned — intoxicated from drugs

stoney — a person who uses drugs regularly

Thai stick — a marijuana cigarette held together by sticks

toke — a single inhalation from a bong, pipe, or marijuana cigarette

trip — the hallucinogenic experience from drugs

tweaked — to feel very nervous as the effect of a drug

upper — drugs that stimulate the central nervous system

vitamin A — LSD
vitamin Q — Quaaludes or methaqualone (drugs)
weed — marijuana

Resources for
Further Information

Resources for
Further Information

GAMES

"The Just Say No Game"
Life Games, Inc.
Available at most toy stores

NATIONAL ORGANIZATIONS

Al-Anon Family Groups
P.O.Box 862
Midtown Station
New York, New York 10018
Telephone: (212) 302-7240

Alcohol, Drug Abuse & Mental
    Health Administration
Department of Health & Human
    Services
5600 Fishers Lane
Room 6C15
Rockville, Maryland 20857
Telephone: (301) 468-2600

Alcoholics Anonymous World
    Services Office, Inc.
P.O.Box 459
Grand Central Station
New York, New York 10163
Telephone: (212) 686-1100

American Council for Drug
    Education (ACDE)
204 Monroe Street
Rockville, Maryland 20850
Telephone: (301) 294-0600

American Medical Association
Department of Health Ed.
535 North Dearborn Street
Chicago, Illinois 60610
Telephone: (312) 645-5000

Compcare
2415 Annapolis Lane
Suite 140
Minneapolis, Minnesota 55441
Telephone: (612) 559-4800

Do It Now Foundation
P.O.Box 21126
Phoenix, Arizona 85036
Telephone: (602) 257-0797

Dream
1991 Lakeland Dr.
Suite B
Jackson, Mississippi 39216
Telephone: (601) 362-9329

Drug Enforcement Administration
1405 I Street NW
Washington, District of Columbia
    20537
Telephone: (202) 633-1000

Drugs Anonymous
P.O. Box 473
Ansonia Station
New York, New York 10023
Telephone: (212) 874-0700

Families in Action
2296 Henderson Mill Rd.
Suite 204
Atlanta, Georgia 30345
Telephone: (404) 934-6364

Families Anonymous Inc.
P.O. Box 528
Van Nuys, Cailfornia 91408
Telephone: (818) 989-7841

Family Life Publications
Box 427
Saluda, North Carolina 28773
Telephone: (704) 749-4971

Food & Drug Administration (FDA)
Consumer Inquiries HFI-10
5600 Fishers Lane
Rockville, Maryland 20857
Telephone: (301) 443-1544

Hazelden Foundation Inc.
15245 Pleasant Valley Road
Box 11
Center City, Minnesota 55012
Telephone: (612) 257-4010

House Select Committee on Narcotics
    Abuse & Control
3287 House Office Building — Annex 2
2nd & D Streets SW
Washington, District of Columbia
    20515
Telephone: (202) 225-3121

Just Say No Club Member's
    Handbook
The Just Say No Foundation
1777 North California Boulevard
Suite 200
Walnut Creek, CA 94596
(800) 258-2766
(415) 939-6666 in California

The Myrin Institute
521 Park Avenue
New York, New York 10021
Telephone: (212) 758-6475

Narcotic Educational Foundation of
    America
5055 Sunset Boulevard
Los Angeles, California 90027
Telephone: (213) 663-5171

Narcotics Anonymous
World Services Inc.
P.O.Box 9999
Van Nuys, California 91409
Telephone: (818) 780-3951

Narcotics Education
Natl. Committee for the Prev. of
    Alcoholism/Drug Dependency
6830 Laurel Street NW
Washington, District of Columbia
    20012-9979
Telephone: (202) 722-6740

National Association on Drug Abuse
    Problems
355 Lexington Avenue
New York, New York 10017
Telephone: (212) 986-1170

National Association of State Alcohol
    & Drug Abuse Directors
444 N. Capitol St NW
Suite 520
Washington, District of Columbia
    20001
Telephone: (202) 783-6868

National Center for Voluntary Action
1111 North 19th Street
Suite 500
Arlington, Virginia 22209
Telephone: (703) 276-0542

National Clearinghouse for Alcohol
  Abuse Information
National Institute on Alcohol Abuse
  and Alcoholism (DHHS)
P.O. Box 2345
Rockville, Maryland 20852
Telephone: (301) 468-2600

National Clearinghouse for Alcohol &
  Drug Abuse Information
  (NCDAI)
5600 Fishers Lane
Rockville, Maryland 20857
Telephone: (301) 443-6500

National Council on Alcoholism
12 West 21st Street
New York, New York 10010
Telephone: (212) 206-6770

Council on Alcoholism
1511 K Street NW
Washington, D.C.
  20005
(202) 737-8122

National Federation of Parents for
  Drug-Free Youth
REACH AMERICA
8730 Georgia Avenue
#200
Silver Springs, Maryland 20910-3604
Telephone: (301) 585-5437

National Self-Help Clearinghouse
Graduate School & University Center-
  CUNY
33 West 42nd Street
New York, New York 10036
Telephone: (212) 840-1259

Pan American Health Organization
Regional Office of the WHO
525 Twenty-third Street, Suite 0027
Washington, District of Columbia
  20012
Telephone: (202) 861-3200

Parent Resource Institute on Drug
  Education (PRIDE)
100 Edgewood Avenue
Suite 1002
Atlanta, Georgia 30303
Telephone: (404) 651-2548

Parents' Association to Neutralize
  Drug and Alcohol Abuse
P.O. Box 314
Annandale, Virginia 22003
(703) 750-9285

Phoenix House Foundation
164 West 74th Street
New York, New York 10023
Telephone: (212) 787-3000

Public Citizen, Inc.
Health Research Group
2000 P Street NW
Washington, District of Columbia
  20036
Telephone: (202) 293-9142

Pyramid
39 Quail Court
Suite 201
Walnut Creek, California 94596
Telephone: (800) 277-0438 or
  (415) 939-6666

Rutgers Center of Alcohol Studies
Publications Division
P.O.Box 969
Piscataway, New Jersey 08855
Telephone: (201) 932-2190

U.S. DHHS Office of Education
Alcohol & Drug Ed. Program
400 Maryland Avenue SW
Washington, District of Columbia
  20202
Telephone: (202) 732-3366

What Works: Schools Without Drugs
  (handbook)
U.S. Department of Education
400 Maryland Avenue SW
Washington, District of Columbia
  20202

STATE ORGANIZATIONS

ALABAMA:

Department of Mental Health
Div. of Mental Illness & Sub. Abuse
    Community Programs
200 Interstate Park Drive
P.O. Box 3710
Montgomery, Alabama 36193
Telephone: (205) 271-9253

ALASKA:

Department of Health & Social
    Services
P.O. Box H-05-F
114 Second Street
Juneau, Alaska 99811-0607
Telephone: (907) 586-6201

ARIZONA:

Alcohol Abuse Section Bureau of
    Community Services
Gov's Office of Substance Abuse
State Capitol, West Wing
1700 West Washington Street
Phoenix, Arizona 85007
Telephone: (602) 255-3456

ARKANSAS:

Office of Alcohol & Drug Abuse
    Prevention
400 Dona Ghey Plaza North
7th and Main Street
Little Rock, Arkansas 72203
Telephone: (501) 682-6656

CALIFORNIA:

Californians for Drug-Free Youth
    Inc.
P.O. Box 1648
Thousand Oaks, California 91360
Telephone: (805) 373-0215

Department of Alcohol & Drug Abuse
    Programs
111 Capitol Mall
Suite 450
Sacramento, California 95814
Telephone: (916) 445-0834

COLORADO:

Alcohol & Drug Abuse Division
Department of Health
4210 East 11th Avenue
Denver, Colorado 80220
Telephone: (303) 331-8201

CONNECTICUT:

Alcohol & Drug Abuse Commission
999 Asylum
3rd Floor
Hartford, Connecticut 06105
Telephone: (203) 566-2089

DELAWARE:

Bureau of Alcoholism & Drug Abuse
Department of Health & Social
    Services
1901 North Dupont Highway
New Castle, Delaware 19720
Telephone: (302) 421-6101 or
    (800) 652-2929

Delaware Youth & Family Center
Division of Child Mental Health
Centre & Faulkland Roads
Wilmington, Delaware 19805
Telephone: (302) 995-8369

DISTRICT OF COLUMBIA:

Department of Human Resources
Mental Health, Alcohol & Drug
    Abuse Services
1300 1st Street N.E.
Room 300
Washington, District of Columbia
    20002
Telephone: (202) 727-0713 or
    727-0740

FLORIDA:

Alcohol & Drug Abuse & Mental
    Health
1317 Winewood Boulevard
Tallahassee, Florida 32301
Telephone: (904) 488-8304

GEORGIA:

Department of Human Services
Division of Mental Health and Mental
    Retardation
Alcohol and Drug Section
878 Peachtree Street NE, Suite 319
Atlanta, Georgia 30334
Telephone: (404) 894-4785

Metropolitan Atlanta Council on
    Alcohol & Drugs
2045 Peachtree Road NE
Suite 605
Atlanta, Georgia 30309
Telephone: (404) 351-1800

HAWAII:

Department of Health Mental Health
    Division
Alcohol & Drug Abuse Branch
1270 Queen Emma, Room 705
P.O.Box 3378
Honolulu, Hawaii 96813
Telephone: (808) 548-4280

IDAHO:

Bureau of Substance Abuse
Department of Health & Welfare
450 West State Street
10th Floor
Boise, Idaho 83720
Telephone: (208) 334-5935

ILLINOIS:

Alcohol & Substance Abuse
100 West Randolph
5th Floor
Chicago, Illinois 60601
Telephone: (312) 917-2735 or
    917-3840

INDIANA:

Division of Addiction Services
Department of Mental Health
117 East Washington Street
Indianapolis, Indiana 46204
Telephone: (317) 232-7816

IOWA:

Department of Substance Abuse
Lucas State Office Bldg.
321 East 12th Street
Des Moines, Iowa 50319
Telephone: (515) 281-3641

KANSAS:

Alcohol & Drug Abuse Services
Section Department of Social
    Rehabilitation Service
300 Southwest Oakley
Topeka, Kansas 66606
Telephone: (913) 296-3925

KENTUCKY:

Alcohol & Drug Branch
Bureau of Health Services DHR
123 Walnut Street
Frankfort, Kentucky 40601
Telephone: (502) 564-4850

LOUISIANA:

Office of Mental Health & Substances
    Abuse
Department of Health & Human
    Resources
655 North 5th Street
P.O.Box 106
Baton Rouge, Louisiana 70829
Telephone: (504) 342-6685

MAINE:

Office of Alcoholism & Drug Abuse
    Prevention (OADAP)
Department of Human Services
State House, Station 11
Augusta, Maine 04333
Telephone: (207) 289-2781

MARYLAND:

Department of Health & Mental
    Hygiene
Alcoholism Control & Drug Abuse
    Administration
201 West Preston Street
Fourth Floor
Baltimore, Maryland 21201
Telephone: (301) 225-6555 or
    225-6910

MASSACHUSETTS:

Department of Public Health
Division of Alcoholism & Drug
    Rehabilitation
150 Treemont Street
Boston, Massachusetts 02111
Telephone: (617) 727-1960 or
    727-8617

MICHIGAN:

Office of Substance Abuse Services
Department of Public Health
3500 North Logan Street
P.O.Box 30195
Lansing, Michigan 48909
Telephone: (517) 335-8810

MINNESOTA:

Department of Public Welfare
Chemical Dependency Program
    Division DPW
444 Lafayette Road
Human Services Bldg.
St. Paul, Minnesota 55155-3823
Telephone: (612) 296-4614

MISSISSIPPI:

Division of Alcohol & Drug Abuse
Department of Mental Health
Room #1101
Robert E. Lee State Office Building
Jackson, Mississippi 32901
Telephone: (601) 359-1297

MISSOURI:

Division of Alcoholism & Drug Abuse
Department of Mental Health
1915 Southridge
P.O.Box 687
Jefferson City, Missouri 65102
Telephone: (314) 751-4942

MONTANA:

Alcohol & Drug Abuse Division
Department of Institutions
1539 11th Avenue
Helena, Montana 59620
Telephone: (406) 444-2827

NEBRASKA:

Department of Public Institutions
Division of Alcoholism and Drug
    Abuse
801 West Van Dorn Street
P.O.Box 94728
Lincoln, Nebraska 68509
Telephone: (402) 471-2851, ext. 5583

Alcohol & Drug Abuse Commission
    of Nebraska
15 Centennial Mall South
Suite 412
Lincoln, Nebraska 68509
Telephone: (402) 474-0930

NEVADA:

Bureau of Alcohol & Drug Abuse
Department of Human Resources
505 East King Street
Room #500
Carson City, Nevada 89710
Telephone: (702) 885-4790

NEW HAMPSHIRE:

Department of Health and Welfare
Office of Alcohol & Drug Abuse
    Prevention
Health & Welfare Building
#6 Hazen Drive
Concord, New Hampshire 03301
Telephone: (603) 271-4627

174

NEW JERSEY:

Alcohol, Narcotic & Drug Abuse
Department of Health
129 East Hanover Street
CN 362
Trenton, New Jersey 08625
Telephone: (609) 292-8949

NEW MEXICO:

Substance Abuse & Behavioral Health
    Service Bureau
Health & Environmental Department
1190 St. Francis Dr., Harold Reynolds
    Bldg.
3rd Floor, Room N-3350
Santa Fe, New Mexico 87503
Telephone: (505) 827-2589

NEW YORK:

Division of Alcoholism and Alcohol
    Abuse
194 Washington Avenue
Albany, New York 12210
Telephone: (518) 474-5417

New York Office of Substance Abuse
    Services
Executive Park South
Box 8200
Albany, New York 12203
Telephone: (518) 457-7629

Addiction Research & Treatment
    Corporation
22 Chapel Street
Brooklyn, New York 11201
Telephone: (718) 260-2900

NORTH CAROLINA:

Department of Human Resources
Alcohol & Drug Abuse Services
325 North Salisbury Street
Albemarle Building, Room 628
Raleigh, North Carolina 27611
Telephone: (919) 733-4670

NORTH DAKOTA:

Division of Alcoholism & Drug Abuse
State Department of Health
1839 East Capital Ave.
Bismarck, North Dakota 58501
Telephone: (701) 224-2769

OHIO:

Department of Health
Division of Alcoholism
246 North High Street
P.O.Box 118
Columbus, Ohio 43266-0588
Telephone: (614) 466-3543

State Methadone Authority
Ohio Department of Mental Health &
    Mental Retardation
170 North High Street
3rd Floor
Columbus, Ohio 43215
Telephone: (614) 466-9023

OKLAHOMA:

Department of Mental Health
Division of Alcoholism & Drug Abuse
    Programs
1200 Northeast 13th
P.O. Box 53277, Capital Station
Oklahoma City, Oklahoma 73152
Telephone: (405) 521-0044 or
    (405) 271-7474

OREGON:

Program for Alcohol & Drug
    Problems
Oregon Mental Health Division
1178 Chemeketa Street N.E.
#102
Salem, Oregon 97310
Telephone: (503) 378-2163

PENNSYLVANIA:

ODAP Pennsylvania Dept. of Health
Bureau of Program Services
   (ENCORE)
Health & Welfare Building, Room 923
P.O. Box 90
Harrisburg, Pennsylvania 17120
Telephone: 1-800-932-0912 or
   (717) 787-9761

RHODE ISLAND:

Division of Substance Abuse
Substance Abuse Administration
   Building
Rhode Island Medical Center
Cranston, Rhode Island 02920
Telephone: (401) 464-2091

SOUTH CAROLINA:

South Carolina Commission on
   Alcohol & Drug Abuse
3700 Forest Drive
Landmark East, Suite 300
Columbia, South Carolina 29204
Telephone: (803) 734-9520

SOUTH DAKOTA:

Department of Health
Division of Alcoholism & Drug Abuse
523 East Capitol
Joe Foss Building
Pierre, South Dakota 57501
Telephone: (605) 773-4806

TENNESSEE:

Division of Alcohol & Drug Abuse
Tennessee Department of Mental
   Health
Doctor's Building
706 Church
Nashville, Tennessee 37219
Telephone: (615) 741-1921

TEXAS:

Commission on Alcholism
Drug Abuse Prevention Division
1705 Guadalupe
Austin, Texas 78701
Telephone: (512) 463-5510

UTAH:

Department of Social Services
Division of Alcoholism & Drugs
120 West North Temple
4th Floor
Salt Lake City, Utah 84103
Telephone: (801) 538-3939

VERMONT:

Agency of Human Services, Alcohol
   & Drug Abuse Division
Department of Social &
   Rehabilitation Services
103 South Main St.
State Office Building
Waterbury, Vermont 05676
Telephone: (802) 241-2170

VIRGINIA:

Department of Mental Health and
   Mental Retardation
Office of Substance Abuse
P.O. Box 1797
109 Governor Street
Richmond, Virginia 23214
Telephone: (804) 786-5313

WASHINGTON:

Bureau of Alcoholism & Substance
   Abuse
Department of Social & Health
   Services
Office Building 2
Mailstop OB-44W
Olympia, Washington 98504
Telephone: (206) 753-5866

WEST VIRGINIA:

Department of Health, Alcoholism &
    Drug Abuse Program
State Capitol
1800 Washington Street East
Building 3, Room 451
Charleston, West Virginia 25305
Telephone: (304) 348-2276

WISCONSIN:

Dept. of Health & Social Services/
    Div. Community Services Bureau
Ofc. of Alcohol & Drug Abuse
One West Wilson Street, Room 434
P.O.Box 7851
Madison, Wisconsin 53707
Telephone: (608) 266-2717

WYOMING:

Substance Abuse Programs
Hathaway Building
Room 350
Cheyenne, Wyoming 82002
Telephone: (307) 777-7115 or
    777-6945

U.S. PROTECTORATES

Mental Health and Substance Abuse
    Agency
P.O.Box 94000
Tauming, Guam 96921
Telephone: 011-671-646-9261

Department of Addiction Control
    Services
21414 Rio Piedras Station
Rio Piedras, Puerto Rico 00928-1414
Telephone: (809) 763-7575

Mental Health Clinic
Government of American Samoa
Pago Pago, American Samoa 96799
Telephone: 011-684-633-5139

Department of Public Health &
    Environmental Services
P.O. Box 409 PK
NPM 56950
Siapan, Trust Territories 96950
Telephone: 011-670-234-8950

Division of Mental Health
Alcoholism & Drug Dependency
6 & 7 Estate Diamond
Christiansted
St. Croix, Virgin Islands 00820
Telephone: (809) 773-8443

CANADIAN ORGANIZATIONS

ALBERTA:

Alberta Alcohol & Drug Abuse
    Commission
7th Floor
10909 Jasper Avenue
Edmonton, Alberta T5J 3M9
Telephone: (403) 427-7301

BRITISH COLUMBIA:

Alcohol and Drug Program
307 West Broadway
Vancouver, British Columbia
    V5Y 1P9
Telephone: (604) 660-6536

177

MANITOBA:

Alcoholism Foundation of Manitoba
1031 Portage Avenue
Winnipeg, Manitoba R3G OR8
Telephone: (204) 944-6200

NEW BRUNSWICK:

Alcoholism Program
Department of Health Library
65 Brunswick Street
P.O. Box 6000
Fredericton, New Brunswick
   E3B 5H1
Telephone: (506) 453-2136

NEWFOUNDLAND:

Alcoholism & Drug Dependency
   Commission
Suite 105 Prince Charles Building
120 Torbay Road
St. John's, Newfoundland A1A 2G8
Telephone: (709) 737-3600

Ministry Department of Health
Main Floor, Confederation Building
West Block
St. John's, Newfoundland A1C 5T7
Telephone: (709) 576-3124

NOVA SCOTIA:

Nova Scotia Commission of Drug
   Dependency
5675 Spring Garden Road
6th Floor
Halifax, Nova Scotia B3J 1H1
Telephone: (902) 424-4270

ONTARIO:

Ministry of Health Promotion and
   Information
80 Grosvonor Street
9th Floor, Hepburn Block
Toronto, Ontario M7A 1S2
Telephone: (416) 965-3101

The Addiction Research Foundation
33 Russell Street
Toronto, Ontario M5S 2S1
Telephone: (416) 595-6000

PRINCE EDWARD ISLAND:

Queen's County Addiction Services of
   Prince Edward Island
P.O. Box 37
Charlottetown, Prince Edward Island
   C1A 7K2
Telephone: (902) 368-4120

Alcohol & Drug Problems Institute
P.O.Box 1832
Charlottetown, Prince Edward Island
   C1A 7N5
Telephone: (902) 892-0461

QUEBEC:

Department of Social Affairs
Information Centre on Alcoholism &
   Other Addictions
1075 Chemin Ste. Foy
Quebec City, Quebec G1S 2M1
Telephone: (418) 643-6024

SASKATCHEWAN:

Alcoholism Commission of
   Saskatchewan
3475 Albert Street
Regina, Saskatchewan S4S 6X6
Telephone: (306) 787-4085

CANADIAN TERRITORIES:

Alcohol & Drug Program
   Commission
Department of Social Services
Government of the Northwest
   Territories
P.O. Box 1320
Yellowknife, Northwest Territories
   X1A 2L9
Telephone: (403) 873-7155

Alcohol & Drug Services
Box 2703
Whitehorse, Yukon Territory
   Y1A 2C6
Telephone: (403) 667-5777

Royal Canadian Mounted Police,
   M Division
N.C.O. in Charge of Drug Awareness
4100 Fourth Avenue
White Horse, Yukon Territory
   Y1A 1H5
Telephone: (403) 667-5584

ENGLAND

Health Educational Commission
287 Haharrow Road
London W93RL, England
Telephone: 011-44-1-286-3275

Narcotics Anonymous
P.O. Box 704
London SW10 ORP, England
Telephone: 011-44-1-351-6794

Institute for the Study of Drug
   Dependence
1-4 Hatton Place
Hatton Garden
London EC1N 8ND, England
Telephone: 011-44-1-430-1993

Release
169 Commercial Street
London E1 6BW, England
Telephone: 011-44-1-377-5905

Mental Health
c/o National Association for Mental
   Health
22 Holly Street
London W1N 2ED, England
Telephone: 011-44-1-637-0741

Department of Addiction to Alcohol
   & Other Drugs
Saint George's Hospital
Blackshore Road
Tooting
London SW17, England
Telephone: 011-44-1-672-1255

Medical Council on Alcoholism
1 Saint Andrew Place
London NW1 4LB, England
Telephone: 011-44-1-487-4445

PUBLICATIONS

American Journal of Drug & Alcohol
   Abuse
Department of Psychiatry UCIMC,
   Building 53
Rt. 81
101 City Drive South
Orange, California 92668
Telephone: (714)

International Journal of the
   Addictions
Marcel Dekker Journals
270 Madison Avenue
New York, New York 10016
Telephone: (212) 696-9000

Drug Abuse & Alcoholism Newsletter
Vista Hill Foundation
3420 Camino del Rio North
Suite 100
San Diego, California 92108
Telephone: (619) 563-1770

Journal of Drug Education
Baywood Publishing Co., Inc.
26 Austin Avenue
Amityville, New York 11701
Telephone: (516) 691-1270

DID YOU BORROW THIS BOOK?

You can have your own personal copy of *How to Drug-Proof Kids*, so you can highlight the important parts and refer to it as needed. To order your personal copy, you can use this order form, or call us at (505) 298-9168 to put it on your MasterCard or VISA.

I understand that if I am not fully satisfied with any book, I may return it at any time for a full refund.

Thank you.

Quantity	Title	Price	Total Price

PAPERBACKS:

_____ *How to Drug-Proof Kids: A Parents' Guide to* $9.95 _____
               Early Prevention

_____ *"Just Say No" Fun Book for Kids* $ 3.95 _____

Shipping Charges: Subtotal _____

$1.50 for the first book, 50 cents for   Shipping _____
   each additional book

[ ] I can't wait 2-4 weeks for book rate. I am   Tax (NM residents add 5 %) _____
   enclosing $2.50 for the first book and $1 for
   each additional book for Air Mail.

                                                                Total _____

[ ] Check enclosed with order.
[ ] Please charge to my credit card.
         [ ] VISA   [ ] MasterCard

Number_____ Exp. Date _____/_____
Signature_____
Ship to: Name _____
Address_____
City_____ State _____ Zip _____

Make your check payable to:
The Think Shop, Inc.
P.O. Box 3754
Albuquerque, NM 87190

BULK ORDERS INVITED

For quantity discounts, call (505) 298-9168, or write The Think Shop at the above address.

THE STEM CELL HOPE

ALICE PARK is the senior science writer for *Time* magazine. She has covered stem cell research for twelve years. She lives in New York City.

Praise for *The Stem Cell Hope*

"A compelling and engrossing narrative about a profoundly important subject that has the potential to transform medicine and affect our lives."
—David Kessler, M.D., former commissioner of the FDA and
New York Times bestselling author of *The End of Overeating*

"Alice Park, one of America's most respected science writers, provides a fascinating perspective on the people, science, politics, promise, and perils of stem cell research. She links the scientific developments to the lives of real people, including scientists and patients, adding a human face to this controversial and rapidly evolving field."
—Steven Nissen, M.D., chairman of cardiovascular medicine,
Cleveland Clinic

"Park infuses a difficult scientific subject with intrigue, passion, and fun—a must-read that is compelling and enjoyable."
—Michael Roizen, M.D., coauthor of the *New York Times* bestselling
YOU series and chief wellness officer of the Cleveland Clinic

"Alice Park's account of the early years of stem cell research gives the reader a front-row seat as the exciting first discoveries were being made by the scientists involved and details the lives of the patients who inspired them. Park's book proves there is truly stem cell hope for all of us, not just hype."
—J. Craig Venter, sequencer of the human genome
and author of *A Life Decoded*

"With *The Stem Cell Hope*, Park eloquently tells the important scientific and political story of stem cells in a clear and engaging voice. The book is a must-read for anyone who wants to understand the important role that stem cell science will play in medicine in coming years."

—Tommy Thompson, former secretary of
the Health and Human Services Department

"*The Stem Cell Hope* provides a thorough and engaging narrative of the challenging path already forged to realize the promise of stem cell research. As we continue the fight to make that promise a reality, this book should serve as mandatory reading for anyone involved in the most important scientific endeavor of our time, and, in particular, provide a reality check for those who wish to stand in the way."

—U.S. Rep. Diana DeGette (CO), the leading congressional advocate
for stem cell research and author of the groundbreaking legislation
that would finally secure this life-saving research for our nation

"*The Stem Cell Hope* is a tour de force of storytelling. Park brings the science alive with her dramatic narrative, while managing the tricky feat of explaining stem cell science with rigor and panache."

—Sharon Begley, bestselling author of
Train Your Mind, Change Your Brain

"*The Stem Cell Hope* tells the life science story of this decade, from the perspective of those who shaped the field. This excellent book is their story. It should be read by anyone who cares about the life sciences or just the preservation and extension of human life."

—Larry Summers, Harvard University